BE HOLY

Be Holy

WARREN W. WIERSBE

ChariotVICTOR
PUBLISHING
A DIVISION OF COOK COMMUNICATIONS

Victor Books is an imprint of ChariotVictor Publishing,
a division of Cook Communications, Colorado Springs, Colorado 80918
Cook Communications, Paris, Ontario
Kingsway Communications, Eastbourne, England

Unless otherwise indicated, all Scripture references are from the *Authorized (King James) Version;* other references are from *The New King James Version (*NKJV). © 1979, 1980, 1982, Thomas Nelson, Inc., Publishers; the *Holy Bible, New International Version®* (NIV). Copyright © 1973, 1978, 1984 by International Bible Society. Used by permission of Zondervan Publishing House. All rights reserved.

Copyediting: Jerry Yamamoto; Barbara Williams
Cover Design: Grace Chan Mallette
Cover Photo: Lewis Kemper

Library of Congress Cataloging-in-Publication Data

Wiersbe, Warren W.
    Be holy / by Warren W. Wiersbe.
      p.   cm.
    ISBN: 1-56476-335-8
    Includes bibliographical references.
    1. Bible. O.T. Leviticus—Criticism, interpretation, etc.
I. Title.
BS1255.2.W54 1994
222'.1307—dc20
                                  94-15649
                                       CIP

---

4   5   6   7   8   9   10   11   Printing/Year   99   98   97

CONTENTS

In March 1995 Warren Wiersbe became Writer in Residence at Cornerstone College in Grand Rapids, Michigan, and Distinguished Professor of Preaching at Grand Rapids Baptist Seminary. He also serves as senior contributing editor in the field of pastoral ministry at Baker Book House.

PREFACE

With prophetic insight, A. W. Tozer wrote many years ago:

> Were some watcher or holy one from the bright world above to come among us for a time with the power to diagnose the spiritual ills of church people, there is one entry which I am quite sure would appear on the vast majority of his reports: *Definite evidence of chronic spiritual lassitude; level of moral enthusiasm extremely low.*[1]

Whatever else the professing Christian church may be known for today — great crowds, expensive buildings, big budgets, political clout — it's not distinguished for its holiness. Bible-believing evangelical Christians make up a sizable minority in the United States, but our presence isn't making much of an impact on society. The salt seems to have lost its saltiness, and the light is so well hidden that the marketplace is quite dark.

Eight times in Scripture, God said to His people, "Be holy, for I am holy!" This is one of the major themes of Leviticus, a book that teaches us how to avoid sin and how to grow in holiness. My prayer is that the study and application of the spiritual principles in Leviticus will make us all more like Jesus Christ and better able to impact this present evil world.

Warren W. Wiersbe

A Suggested Outline of the Book of Leviticus

Theme: The holiness of God—"Be holy, for I am holy"
Theme verses: Leviticus 11:44-45

I. Holy Offerings—1–7
   1. Laws for the worshipers—1:1–6:7
   2. Laws for the priests—6:8–7:38

II. A Holy Priesthood—8–10, 21–22
   1. Consecration—8–9
   2. Admonition—10
   3. Qualification—21–22

III. A Holy Nation—11–17
   1. Clean and unclean food—11
   2. Childbirth—12
   3. Diseases and defilement—13–15
   4. The Day of Atonement—16–17

IV. A Holy Land—18–20, 23–27
   1. Immorality—18
   2. Idolatry—19
   3. Capital offenses—20
   4. Annual feasts—23
   5. Blasphemy—24
   6. Sabbatical Year—25
   7. Blessings and cursings—26–27

The Most Important Thing in the World

W e will stand and sing hymn 325," announced the worship leader, " 'Take Time to Be Holy.' We will sing verses one and four."

If I had been sitting with the congregation instead of on the platform, I might have laughed out loud. Imagine a Christian congregation singing "Take Time to Be Holy" *and not even taking time to sing the entire song!* If we can't take the time (less than four minutes) to sing a song about holiness, we're not likely to take time to devote ourselves to "perfecting holiness in the fear of God" (2 Cor. 7:1).

Happiness, not holiness, is the chief pursuit of most people today, including many professed Christians. They want Jesus to solve their problems and carry their burdens, but they don't want Him to control their lives and change their character. It doesn't disturb them that eight times in the Bible, God said to His people, "Be holy, for I am holy,"[1] *and He means it.*

"He that sees the beauty of holiness, or true moral good," wrote Jonathan Edwards, "sees the greatest and most important thing in the world."

Have you ever thought of personal holiness—likeness to Jesus Christ—as *the most important thing in the world?*

In God's kingdom, holiness isn't a luxury; it's a necessity. "Follow peace with all men, and holiness, without which no man shall see the Lord" (Heb. 12:14). Yes, God wants His children to be happy, but true happiness begins with holiness. "Blessed are they which do hunger and thirst after righteousness; for they shall be filled" (Matt. 5:6). "If I had my choice of all the blessings I can conceive of," said Charles Spurgeon, "I would choose perfect conformity to the Lord Jesus, or, in one word, holiness." Would you make the same choice?

Leviticus tells new Testament Christians how to appreciate holiness and appropriate it into their everyday lives. The word *holy* is used 91 times in Leviticus, and words connected with *cleansing* are used 71 times. References to *uncleanness* number 128. There's no question what this book is all about.

"But wasn't the Book of Leviticus written for the priests and Levites in ancient Israel?" you may ask; and the answer is, "Yes." But the lessons in Leviticus aren't limited to the Jews in ancient Israel. The spiritual principles in this book apply to Christians in the church today. The key verses of Leviticus — "Be holy, for I am holy" (Lev. 11:44-45) — are applied to the New Testament church in 1 Peter 1:15-16; and the Book of Leviticus itself is quoted or referred to over 100 times in the New Testament. Since *all Scripture* was given by inspiration of God (2 Tim. 3:16), then *all Scripture* is profitable for God's people to use in developing godly lives. Jesus said that we should live by *every* word that God has given us (Matt. 4:4), and that includes Leviticus.

The Book of Leviticus explains five basic themes that relate to the life of holiness: a holy God; a holy priesthood; a holy people; a holy land; and a holy Savior.

1. A holy God

What is "holiness"? Contrary to what you may hear today in some sermons and popular religious songs, the emphasis in the Bible is on the *holiness of God* and not on the love of God. "Love is central in God," wrote American theologian Augustus H. Strong, "but holiness is central in love."[2] God's love is a *holy* love, for the Bible states that "God is light" (1 John 1:5) as well as "God is love" (4:8, 16). Love without holiness would be a monstrous thing that could destroy God's perfect law, while holiness without love would leave no hope for the lost sinner. Both are perfectly balanced in the divine nature and works of God.

God's holiness isn't simply the absence of defilement, a negative thing. The holiness of God is positive and active. It's God's perfect nature at work in accomplishing God's perfect will.

The Hebrew word for "holy" that Moses used in Leviticus means "that which is set apart and marked off, that which is different." The Sabbath was holy because God set it apart for His people (Ex. 16:23). The priests were holy because they were set apart to minister to the Lord (Lev. 21:7-8). Their garments were holy and could not be duplicated for common use (Ex. 28:2). The tithe that the people brought was holy (Lev. 27:30). Anything that God said was holy had to be treated differently from the common things of life in the Hebrew camp. In fact, the camp of Israel was holy, because the Lord dwelt there with His people (Deut. 23:14).

Our English word "holy" comes from the Old English word *halig* which means "to be whole, to be healthy." What health is to the body, holiness is to the inner person. The related word "sanctify" comes from the Latin *sanctus* which means "consecrated, sacred, blameless." We use the word "sanctification" to describe the process of growing to become more like Christ, and "holy" to describe the result of that process.[3]

How does God reveal His holiness? The religion of the nations in Canaan was notoriously immoral and involved worshiping idols and consorting with temple prostitutes, both male and female. (The mythological deities of Greece and Rome weren't much better.) For this reason, God commanded His people to stay away from their altars and shrines and to refuse to learn their ways (Ex. 23:20-33; Deut. 7:1-11). In many ways, God made it clear to His people that He was a *holy* God.

To begin with, He gave them *a holy law* that contained both promises and penalties, of which the Ten Commandments are the essence (Ex. 20:1-17). God's statutes and ordinances governed the daily life of the people and told them what was right and wrong, what was clean and unclean, and what the penalties were for those who deliberately disobeyed.

At Sinai, God revealed His *holy presence.* "And all the people saw the thunderings, and the lightnings, and the noise of the trumpet, and the mountain smoking; and when the people saw it, they removed, and stood afar off" (20:18; see 19:14-25). He also revealed His holy power and presence when He judged the gods of Egypt (12:12), when He opened the Red Sea and destroyed the Egyptian army (14:13–15:21), and when He did miraculous works for Israel in the wilderness.

God is "glorious in holiness" (15:11), and His glory dwelt in the holy of holies in both the tabernacle (40:34-38) and the temple (1 Kings 8:10). The presence of the cloud of glory and the pillar of fire reminded Israel that Jehovah was a holy God and "a consuming fire" (Deut. 4:24; Heb. 12:29). In fact, the very structure of the tabernacle declared the holiness of God: the fence around the tent, the brazen altar where the blood was shed, the laver where the priests washed their hands and feet, and the veil that kept everybody but the high priest out of the holy of holies.

The whole sacrificial system declared to Israel that "the wages of sin is death" (Rom. 6:23) and "the soul who sins shall die" (Ezek. 18:4, NKJV). God hates sin, but because He loves sinners and wants to forgive them, He provides a substitute to die in the sinner's place. All of this is a picture of the promised Savior who laid down His life for the sins of the world.

You could never call any of the heathen deities "holy." But "Holy One of Israel" is one of the repeated names of Jehovah in Scripture. It's used thirty times in Isaiah alone.

In declaration and demonstration, Jehovah made it clear to the people of Israel that He is a holy God, righteous in all His works and just in all His judgments.

2. A holy priesthood

The Jewish priesthood belonged only to the tribe of Levi. Levi, the founder of the tribe, was the third son of Jacob and Leah (Gen. 29:34; 35:23) and the father of Gershom, Kohath, and Merari (46:11). Since Kohath's son Amram was the father of Aaron, Moses, and Miriam (Num. 26:58-59), Aaron, Moses, and Miriam belonged to the tribe of Levi.

Aaron was the first high priest and his male descendants became priests, with the firstborn son in each generation inheriting the high priesthood. (Every priest was a Levite, but not every Levite was a priest.) The rest of the men in the tribe of Levi (the "Levites") were assigned to serve as assistants to the priests. The Levites were the substitutes for the firstborn males in Israel, all of whom had to be dedicated to the Lord (Ex. 13:1-16; Num. 3:12-13, 44-51). To facilitate their ministry, David eventually divided the thousands of Levites into twenty-four "courses" (1 Chron. 23:6).

The name "Leviticus" comes from "Levi" and means "pertaining to the Levites." Actually, the Levites are mentioned in only one verse in this book (Lev. 25:32); the regulations in Leviticus pertain primarily to the priests. Of course, as assistants to the priests, the Levites would have to know what the Lord wanted done in the ministry of His house.

God insisted that the priests be holy men, set apart for His service alone. Not only must they come from the tribe of Levi, but also they must not have any physical defects or marry women whom God disapproved (chaps. 21–22). They were set apart in an elaborate ceremony that involved their being bathed in water and marked by oil and blood (chap. 8). The high priest was anointed with special oil. The priests wore special garments, and special laws that didn't apply to the common people governed their lives. In every way, the priests demonstrated the fact that they were set apart and therefore holy to the Lord.

The Levites were in charge of the sanctuary, and during the wilderness years of Israel's wanderings they carried the tent and its furnishings from place to place (Num. 1:47-54). They were also responsible to guard God's sanctuary (1 Chron. 9:19), to teach the people the Law (Deut. 33:8-11; Neh. 8:7-9), and to lead the worshipers in praising God (1 Chron. 28:28-32).

Only a holy priesthood could approach God's altar and be acceptable to serve God. If the priests weren't dressed properly (Ex. 28:39-43), if they didn't wash properly (30:20-21), or if they tried to serve while unclean (Lev. 22:9), they were in danger of death. If the Levites were careless with the tabernacle furnishings, they too might die (Num. 4:15, 20). The high priest wore a golden plate at the front of his turban on which was the inscription, "Holiness to the Lord" (Ex. 28:36); and he dared not do anything that would violate that inscription. He could be serving in the holy of holies in the tabernacle and still be in danger of death (Lev. 16:3).

Every true believer in Jesus Christ is a priest of God, with the privilege of offering spiritual sacrifices through Jesus Christ (1 Peter 2:5, 9). In the Old Testament, God's people *had* a priesthood; but in the New Testament, God's people *are* a priesthood (Rev. 1:6). Through faith in Christ, we've been washed (1 Cor. 6:9-11), clothed in His righteousness

(2 Cor. 5:21), anointed by the Spirit (1 John 2:20, 27) and given access into His presence (Heb. 10:19-20).

3. A holy people

God's purpose for Israel was that the nation be "a kingdom of priests and a holy nation" (Ex. 19:6, NKJV). Everything in the life of the Old Testament Jew was either "holy" (set apart for God's exclusive use) or "common," and the "common" things were either "clean" (the people could use them) or "unclean" (it was forbidden to use them). The Jews had to be careful to avoid what was unclean; otherwise, they would find themselves "cut off from the people" until they had gone through the proper ceremony to be made clean again.

The laws governing marriage, birth, diets, personal cleanliness, the quarantine of diseased persons, and the burial of the dead, while they certainly involved hygienic benefits to the nation, were all reminders that God's people couldn't live any way they pleased. Because they were God's chosen people, the Jews had to learn to put a difference "between holy and unholy, and between unclean and clean" (Lev. 10:10). They must not live like the godless nations around them.

When you read Leviticus 11–17, you will see how the Jewish people were distinguished by their diet, their treatment of newborn babies (and the mothers) and of dead bodies, and their handling of people with diseases and sores. Once a year, on the Day of Atonement (chap. 16), the nation was reminded that Jehovah was a holy God and that the shed blood was the only way of cleansing the people.

God's church is supposed to be "a holy nation" in this present evil world, to "declare the praises of Him who called you out of darkness into his wonderful light" (1 Peter 2:9, NIV). The Greek word translated "declare" means "to tell out, to advertise." The holy nation of Israel in Canaan, with its holy priesthood, revealed to the pagan nations around them the glories and excellencies of Jehovah, the true and living God. The church in today's world has the same privilege and responsibility. When Israel started to live like the pagans, they robbed God of His glory; and the Lord had to chasten them.

4. A holy land

The people belonged to the Lord, because He had redeemed them from Egypt to be His very own; and the land belonged to the Lord, and He gave it to Israel with the stipulation that they do nothing to defile it. A holy God wants His holy people to live in a holy land.

In Leviticus 18–27, the word "land" is used sixty-eight times. In these chapters, Moses named the sins that defile the land and invite divine judgment: immorality (chap. 18); idolatry (chap. 19); capital crimes (chap. 20); blasphemy (chap. 23); and refusing to give the land its rest (chap. 25). Unfortunately, the Jewish people committed all these sins and more; and God had to chasten them by allowing Babylon to destroy Jerusalem and take the people captive (2 Chron. 36:14-21).

The nations of the world today don't have the same covenant relationship to God that Israel has, but they are still responsible to obey His moral law and use His gifts wisely (Amos 1–2). I can't speak about other nations, but I believe my own beloved land is guilty of abusing God's gifts and refusing to obey God's laws, and is therefore ripe for judgment. The very sins that God condemns — murder, deceit, immorality, violence, greed, and blasphemy — are the very things that entertain the masses, whether it's on television or in movies or books. Take the violence and vice out of entertainment and many people won't pay to see it.

God even gave His people an annual calendar to follow to help them appreciate His gifts and use them for His glory (chaps. 23, 25). Until after the Babylonian Captivity, the Jews were primarily an agricultural people; and the calendar of feasts was tied directly to the annual harvests. The Sabbatical Years and the Year of Jubilee not only helped conserve the land, they also helped regulate the economy of the nation. The ungodly nations could just look at the land of Israel and see that Jehovah was blessing His people and caring for them!

5. A holy Savior

To study the Bible and not see Jesus Christ is to miss the major theme of the book (Luke 24:47). The law was "a shadow of good things to come" (Heb. 10:1). Especially in the levitical sacrifices and the priestly ministry do we see the person and work of Jesus Christ vividly portrayed.

No amount of good works or religious efforts can make a sinner holy. Only the blood of Jesus Christ can cleanse us from our sins (1 John 1:7), and only the risen glorified Savior can intercede for us at the throne of God as our Advocate (2:1) and high priest (Heb. 8:1; Rom. 8:34). What the Old Testament Jews saw only in shadows, believers today see in the bright light of Jesus Christ.

Just as the nation of Israel had to beware of that which was unclean and defiling, so must believers today "cleanse [themselves] from all filthiness of the flesh and spirit, perfecting holiness in the fear of God" (2 Cor. 7:1). God wants us to be a "holy priesthood" and a "holy nation" so that we will advertise His virtues and glorify His name (1 Peter 2:5, 9).

On Sunday morning, January 24, 1861, Charles Haddon Spurgeon closed his sermon at the Metropolitan Tabernacle with these words:

An unholy Church! It is of no use to the world, and of no esteem among men. Oh, it is an abomination, hell's laughter, heaven's abhorrence. And the larger the Church, the more influential, the worst nuisance does it become, when it becomes dead and unholy. The worst evils which have ever come upon the world, have been brought upon her by an unholy Church.

Eight times in His Word, the Lord says, "Be holy, for I am holy!" Are we listening?

The Sacrifices and the Savior

L et's review what Israel had been doing prior to the giving of the instructions found in the Book of Leviticus.

About ten weeks after their deliverance from Egypt, the Israelites arrived at Mt. Sinai (Ex. 19:1). There God declared His law and gave Moses the instructions for building the tabernacle. Moses erected the tabernacle on the first day of the first month of the *second* year of Israel's liberation (40:17), so that what you read in Exodus 16–40 covers about nine months (see Num. 9:1-5).

The Book of Numbers opens with a census being taken on the first day of the *second* month of the second year (Num. 1:1), which means that what's recorded in Leviticus covers about one month. The tabernacle was ready for use, and now God gave the priests the instructions they needed for offering the various sacrifices.

Six basic offerings could be brought to the tabernacle altar. When worshipers wanted to express *commitment to God*, they brought the burnt offering, and possibly along with it the grain or meal ("meat," KJV) offering and the drink offering (see Num. 15:1-10). These offerings speak of total dedication to the Lord. The fellowship ("peace," KJV) offering has to do with *communion with God,* and the sin offering and the guilt ("trespass," KJV) offerings deal with *cleansing from God.* Each of these offerings met a specific need in the life of the worshiper and also expressed some truth about the person and work of Jesus Christ, God's perfect sacrifice.

The shedding of animal blood couldn't change a person's heart or take away sin (Heb. 10:1-4). However, God did state that the sins of the worshiper were forgiven (Lev. 4:20, 26, 31, 35; 5:10, 13, 16, 18; 6:7); and He did this on the basis of the sacrifice of Jesus Christ on the cross (Heb. 10:5-14).[1]

Like some people in churches today, Jewish worshipers could merely go through the motions at the altar, without putting their heart into it; but this meant that God had not truly forgiven them (Pss. 50:8-14; 61:16-17; Isa. 1:10-20; Micah 6:6-8). God doesn't want our sacrifices; He wants obedience from our hearts (1 Sam. 15:22).

The sacrifices described in Leviticus 1–7 remind us of the basic spiritual needs we have as God's people: commitment to God, communion with God, and cleansing from God.

1. Commitment to God (Lev. 1–2; 6:8-23)

The burnt offering (1:1-17; 6:8-13) was the basic sacrifice that expressed devotion and dedication to the Lord. When we surrender ourselves to the Lord, we put "all on the altar" (1:9) and hold back nothing. The New Testament parallel is Romans 12:1-2, where God's people are challenged to be *living* sacrifices, wholly yielded to the Lord.

The ritual of the offering was spelled out by the Lord and could not be varied. The sacrifice had to be a male animal from the herd (Lev. 1:3-10) or the flock (vv. 10-14), or it could be a bird (vv. 14-17);[2] and the worshiper had to bring the sacrifice to the door of the tabernacle, where a fire was constantly burning on a brazen altar (6:13). The priest examined the sacrifice to make sure it was without blemish (22:20-24), for we must give our very best to the Lord (see Mal. 1:6-14). Jesus Christ was a sacrifice "without blemish and without spot" (1 Peter 1:19), who gave Himself in total dedication to God (John 10:17; Rom. 5:19; Heb. 10:10).

Except when birds were sacrificed, the offerer laid a hand on the sacrifice (Lev. 1:4), an action which symbolized two things: (1) the offerer's identification with the sacrifice and (2) the transfer of something to the sacrifice. In the case of the burnt offering, the offerer was saying, "Just as this animal is wholly given to God on the altar, so I wholly give myself to the Lord." With the sacrifices that involved the shedding of blood, the laying on of hands meant the worshiper was symbolically transferring sin and guilt to the animal who died in the place of the sinner. Even the burnt offering made atonement for the offerer (v. 4).

The offerer then killed the animal, and the priest caught the blood in a basin and sprinkled the blood on the sides of the altar (vv. 5, 11). The priest, not the offerer, killed the bird and its blood was drained out on the side of the altar, and its body burned in the fire on the altar (vv. 15-17). The dead body of the bull, lamb, or goat was dismembered, and the parts washed. Then all of it but the hide was laid in order on the wood[3] and burned in the fire. The hide was given to the priest (7:8).

The significance of the offering is seen in the repetition of the phrases "before the Lord" and "unto the Lord," which are found seven times in this first chapter of Leviticus (vv. 2-3, 5, 9, 13-14, 17). The transaction at the altar wasn't between the offerer and his conscience, or the offerer and the nation, or even the offerer and the priest; it was between the offerer and the Lord. Had the worshiper taken the offering to one of the pagan temples, it might have pleased the heathen priest and his people, but it would not have brought the blessing of the Lord.

The phrase "sweet savour" is used three times in this chapter (vv. 9, 13, 17) and eight times in chapters 1–3, and it means "a fragrant aroma." Since God is spirit, He doesn't have a body, but physical terms are used in Scripture to depict God's actions and responses. In this case, God is pictured as smelling a fragrant aroma and being pleased with it (Gen. 8:21; Lev. 26:31). When Jesus died on the cross, His sacrifice was a "sweet-smelling fragrance" to the Lord (Eph. 5:2); and our offerings to God should follow that example (Phil. 4:18).

The "law of the burnt offering" is found in Leviticus 6:9-13. God instructed the priests to keep the fire burning on the altar, to remove the ashes from the altar, and then to take them to a clean place outside the camp. It's likely that God originally ignited this fire when the priests were dedicated and began their ministry (9:24).[4] Because the ashes were holy, they couldn't be disposed of at the camp's refuse heap, but had to be taken to a place that was ceremonially clean. Even the crop of the bird was put with the ashes (1:16) and not treated like rubbish.

The meal offering (2:1-16; 6:14-23; 7:9-10)[5] could be presented at the altar in one of five forms: fine flour, oven-baked cakes, cakes baked in a pan, cakes baked in a frying pan (on a griddle), or crushed roasted heads of new grain. These cakes would resemble our modern baked pie crust or pizza dough. The officiating priest put only a portion of the offering on the altar—the "memorial portion" for the Lord—where it was consumed in the fire; and the rest of the offering went to the priests for their own personal use. Only the males in the family could eat it, and they had to do it in the holy place of the tabernacle (6:16, 18), and with unleavened bread (v. 17). The only meal offering that was not eaten was the one presented each morning and evening by the high priest's son, who would succeed him in office (vv. 19-23). Twice a day,

God reminded His priests that they should maintain purity and integrity as they served Him.

Since grain represents the fruit of our labor, the meal offering was one way for the Jews to dedicate to God that which He had enabled them to produce. The frankincense that was burned with the memorial portion represents prayer (Ps. 141:2; Rev. 5:8), a reminder of the petition "Give us this day our daily bread" (Matt. 6:11). But the meal offering was not presented alone; it accompanied one of the sacrifices that involved the shedding of blood. Our hard work can never purchase salvation or earn the blessing of God; for apart from the shedding of blood, there is no forgiveness of sin (Heb. 9:22).[6] But those who have been saved by faith in the shed blood of Christ may dedicate to the Lord what He has enabled them to produce.

This offering represents Jesus Christ as the Bread of Life (John 6:32ff), the perfect One who nourishes our inner person as we worship Him and ponder His Word. This explains why God laid down such strict conditions for the offerer to meet before the meal offering would be accepted. The offering had to be accompanied with oil (Lev. 2:1-2, 4, 6, 15), either poured on it or mingled with it, a picture of the Holy Spirit of God, who was given to Christ without measure (John 3:34). It also had to include salt (Lev. 2:13; Matt. 5:13), which speaks of our Lord's purity of character. Jesus compared Himself to a grain of wheat (John 12:23-25), and He was crushed ("fine flour") and put through the furnace of suffering that He might save us from our sins.

Leaven (yeast) and honey were prohibited from being included in the meal offering (Lev. 2:11). The Jews would associate leaven with evil because of the Passover rules (Ex. 12:19-20; see Luke 12:1; 1 Cor. 5:8), and certainly there was no sin in Jesus Christ. Honey is the sweetest thing nature produces, but our Lord's perfect character was divine and not from this world. The fact that yeast and honey both ferment may also be a factor.

The drink offering (Num. 15:1-13) is mentioned in Leviticus 23:13, 18, and 37; but its "laws" are not explained there. Like the meal offering, the drink offering was presented after the animal sacrifices had been put on the altar and was a required part of the sacrifice (see Num. 29:6, 11, 18-19, and so on). "The fourth part of a hin of wine" (15:5) would be about a quart of liquid. Neither the offerer nor the priest drank the wine, because all of it was poured out on the altar. Note that the more expensive sacrifices required a larger amount of wine for the drink offering.

The burnt offering, the meal offering, and the drink offering all represent dedication to God and commitment to Him and His work. The pouring out of the wine was a symbol of life being poured out in dedication to God. On the cross, Jesus was "poured out like water" (Ps. 22:14) and "poured out His life unto death" (Isa. 53:12, NIV). Paul saw himself poured out like a drink offering on behalf of the Philippians, joining in their sacrifice (Phil. 2:17); and in the Roman prison, he was already "being poured out like a drink offering" (2 Tim. 4:6, NIV) as he anticipated his martyrdom.

2. Communion with God (Lev. 3; 7:11-38)

There are several distinctive features about the peace offering or fellowship offering that should be noted. For one thing, the offerer could bring a female animal, something not permitted for the other animal sacrifices. If the offering was not in fulfillment of a vow, the sacrifice could have some defects and still be accepted (Lev. 22:23). After all, it was basically going to be used as food for the priests and the offerer's family; and those defects wouldn't matter.

That leads to our third distinctive feature: the fellowship offering is the only offering that was shared with the worshipers. After the priest had completed the sacrifice, a large portion of the meat went to him; the rest went to the offerer, who could then enjoy a feast with his family and friends. Since the Jews didn't often slaughter their precious animals for meat, a dinner of beef or lamb would be a special occasion. At the dedication of the temple, Solomon sacrificed 142,000 peace offerings and the people feasted for two weeks (1 Kings 8:62-66).

In the East, to eat with people is to make them your friends and allies. It means the end of hostilities, as with Jacob and his father-in-law Laban (Gen. 31:54), or the sealing of friendship, as with Israel and Jethro and his people (Ex. 18:12). In the church today, the Lord's Supper, or Eucharist, is a simple meal that shows the unity of God's family (1 Cor. 10:16-18; 11:18-34). That's why it's called "the Communion."

The peace offering meal, however, meant more than the enjoyment of good food and fellowship with loved ones. It was also an expression of joyful thanksgiving that the worshiper was at peace with God and in communion with God. He might be giving thanks for some unexpected blessing God sent him (Lev. 7:11-15); or perhaps he had made a vow to God, and God had answered his prayers; or maybe he was just thankful to God for everything God did for him and wanted to let everybody know (vv. 16-18). The fellowship offering emphasized the fact that the forgiveness of sins resulted in communion with God and with God's people.

Leviticus 7:11-38 lays down the conditions for the feast, what the people ate, what the priests ate, and what must be done with the leftovers. The blood and the fat[7] were given to God and were never to be used as common food. (There are also good hygienic reasons for this rule.) Anybody who was defiled was forbidden to come to the feast and was "cut off" from their people (vv. 20-21, 25, 27; see 17:4, 9-10, 14; 18:29; 19:8; 20:3, 5-6, 17-18; 23:29). In the case of a Sabbath-breaker, being "cut off" meant death (Ex. 31:12-14; Num. 15:32-36); but we're not sure every violation of the laws of the offerings was a capital crime. In some cases, "cut off from his people" could mean being sent "outside the camp" until the person followed God's instructions for cleansing (Lev. 15).

On the cross, Jesus Christ purchased reconciliation with God (2 Cor. 5:16-21) and peace with God (Col. 1:20) for all who will trust Him; and we can have fellowship with God and other believers because of His shed blood (1 John 1:5–2:2). We "feast" on Christ when we feed on His Word and appropriate for ourselves all that He is to us and has done for us. Instead of bringing animals, we offer God "the sacrifice of thanksgiving" (Ps. 116:17) and "the sacrifice of praise" (Heb. 13:15), from pure hearts that are grateful for His mercies.

3. Cleansing from God (Lev. 4–5; 6:1-7, 24-30; 7:1-10)
The sin offering and the guilt (or trespass) offering were very much alike and were even governed by the same law (7:1-10). Generally speaking, the guilt offering was for individual sins that affected people and property and for which restitution could be made, while the sin offering focused on some violation of the law that was done without deliberate intent. The trespass offering emphasized the *damage* done to others by the offender, while the sin offering emphasized the offender's *guilt* before God. The priest would examine the offender and determine which sacrifice was needed.

The repeated phrase "through ignorance" (4:2, 13, 22, 27; 5:15) means, not that the sinners were ignorant of the law, but that they were ignorant of having violated the law. They had become defiled or disobedient and didn't realize it. However, ignorance doesn't cancel guilt. "Though he wist it not, yet is he guilty" (v. 17; see vv. 1-5 for examples of the sins involved).[8] Once their sin was known, it had to be confessed and dealt with. David used this same word when he prayed,

"Cleanse Thou me from secret faults" (Ps. 19:12), that is, "sins I don't know about in my own life."

No sacrifice was provided for people who committed "high-handed" deliberate sins in the full light of the law of God (Num. 15:30-36). When David took Bathsheba and then had her husband murdered (2 Sam. 11–12), he sinned deliberately with his eyes wide open. Therefore, he knew that his only hope was the mercy of God (Ps. 51:1, 11, 16-17). Being king, he could have brought thousands of sacrifices, but they would not have been "sacrifices of righteousness" (v. 19).

The sin offering (Lev. 4:1–5:13; 6:24-30)[9] had to be brought to the Lord no matter who the sinner was; and the higher the sinner's position in the nation, the more expensive the sacrifice. The greater the privilege, the greater the responsibility and the consequences. If the high priest sinned, he had to bring a young bullock (Lev. 4:1-12). If the whole congregation sinned, they also had to bring a bullock (vv. 13-22). A ruler brought a male kid of the goats (vv. 22-26), while one of the "common people" ("a member of the community," NIV) brought a female kid of the goats or a female lamb (vv. 27-35). A poor person could bring a dove or a pigeon, and a very poor person could bring a nonbloody sacrifice of fine flour (5:7-13).

Whatever animal was brought, the offender had to identify with the sacrifice by laying hands on it. When the whole nation sinned, it was the elders who did this (4:15); for as leaders, they were responsible before God to oversee the spiritual life of the people. The animal was slain, and the blood presented to God. In the case of the high priest and the nation, some of the blood was sprinkled before the veil and applied to the horns of the altar of incense in the holy place; and the rest was poured out at the base of the altar. This reminded the nation that the sins of leaders had far greater consequences. The blood of the sacrifices brought by the leaders or the common people was applied to the horns of the brazen altar at the door of the tabernacle.

Note that while the fat of the sacrifice was burned on the altar, the body of the sacrifice was burned in a clean place outside the camp (vv. 8-12, 21). Why? For one thing, it made a distinction between the sin offering and the burnt offering so that the worshipers wouldn't be confused as they watched. But even more, it reminded the people that the sins of the high priest and the whole congregation would pollute the whole camp; and the sin offering was too holy to remain in an unholy camp. Finally, according to Hebrews 13:10-13, this was a picture of our Lord Jesus Christ who died "outside the city gate . . . outside the camp" as our sin offering (vv. 12-13, NIV).

The result of this ritual was forgiveness (Lev. 4:20, 26, 31, 35; see 5:10, 13; 6:7). As I mentioned before, even though the sacrifice of animals can't take away sin or change the human heart, the sacrifices pointed to the perfect Sacrifice, Jesus Christ (Heb. 10:1-15). He is our sin offering (Isa. 53:4-6, 12; Matt. 26:28; 2 Cor. 5:21; 1 Peter 2:24).

The trespass offering (Lev. 5:14–6:17; 7:1-10) was needed for two kinds of sins: sins against "the holy things of the Lord" (5:15) and against one's neighbor (6:1-7). The first category included offenses that involved sacrifices to God, vows, celebration of the special days, and so on, while examples of the second category are given in verses 2-3.

The ritual involved the sinner confessing the sin (Num. 5:7), restoring the property involved or its equivalent in money, paying a fine equivalent to 20 percent of the value of the damaged property, and sacrificing a ram to the Lord (Lev. 5:15, 18). The priest valued the ram to make sure of its worth, lest the offender try to atone for his or her sins by giving the Lord something cheap. The restitution and fine were first given to the priest so he would know it was permissible to offer the sacrifice (6:10). If the offended party wasn't available to receive the property or money, then it could be paid to one of the relatives; if no relative was available, it remained with the priest (Num. 5:5-10).

The trespass offering illustrates the solemn fact that *it is a very costly thing for people to commit sin and for God to cleanse sin.* Our sins hurt God and hurt others. True repentance will always bring with it a desire for restitution. We will want to make things right with God and with those whom we've sinned against. Forgiveness comes only because of the death of an innocent substitute. The passage in Isaiah 53:10 states clearly that when Jesus died on the cross, God made His Son "a guilt offering" (NIV). The penalty we should have paid, He paid for us!

We haven't been able to probe into the details of these offerings; but what we have studied should make us realize the awfulness of sin, the seriousness of confession and restitution, the graciousness of God in forgiving those who trust Jesus Christ, and the marvelous love of our Savior in His willingness to die for undeserving people like us.

Jesus provides all that we need. He is our burnt offering, and we must yield ourselves wholly to Him. He is our meal offering, the seed crushed and put through the fire, that we might have the bread of life; and we must feed upon Him. He is our drink offering who poured Himself out in sacrifice and service, and we must pour ourselves out for Him and for others. He is our fellowship offering, making life a joyful feast instead of a painful famine. He is our sin offering and our guilt offering, for He bore our sins on His body (1 Peter 2:24) and paid the full price for our sins (1:18-19).

The nation of Israel had to offer six different sacrifices in order to have a right relationship with God, but Jesus Christ "offered one sacrifice for sins forever" (Heb. 10:12) and took care of our sin problem completely.

Do *you* believe that Jesus Christ died for all your sins and paid your full debt? Can you say with Mary, "My soul magnifies the Lord, and my spirit has rejoiced in God my Savior"? (Luke 1:46-47, NKJV) If not, then trust Him today; if you have trusted Him, share the good news with others.

"Your faith has saved you," Jesus said to a repentant sinner. "Go in peace" (Luke 7:50, NKJV).

What wonderful words to hear!

THREE

A Kingdom of Priests

Under the Old Covenant, God's people *had* a priesthood; under the New Covenant, God's people *are* a "holy priesthood" and a "royal priesthood" (1 Peter 2:5, 9). Every believer in Jesus Christ can say with the Apostle John: "To Him who loved us and washed us from our sins in His own blood, and has made us kings and priests to His God and Father, to Him be glory and dominion, forever and ever" (Rev. 1:5-6, NKJV).

God's desire was that the entire nation of Israel be "a kingdom of priests, and a holy nation" (Ex. 19:6), but they failed Him and became "a sinful nation, a people laden with iniquity" (Isa. 1:4). One reason the nation decayed morally and spiritually was because the leaders failed to be holy and obedient as God commanded. God finally had to send Babylon to chasten Israel "for the sins of her prophets, and the iniquities of her priests" (Lam. 4:13). "A horrible and shocking thing has happened in the land," said Jeremiah. "The prophets prophesy lies, the priests rule by their own authority, and My people love it this way. But what will you do in the end?" (Jer. 5:30-31, NIV)

God wants His church today to be "a holy nation, a people

belonging to God, that [they] may declare the praises of Him who called [them] out of darkness into His wonderful light" (1 Peter 2:9, NIV). The Jewish priests were a privileged people, yet they despised their privileges and helped lead the nation into sin. Even after the Jews returned to their land from Babylon and established their worship again, the priests didn't give God their best; and God had to rebuke them (Mal. 1:6–2:17).

Leviticus 8–10 describes the eight-day ordination ceremony for the high priest Aaron and his sons. As God's chosen priests, they had to accept three solemn responsibilities: submitting to God's authority (chap. 8), revealing God's glory (chap. 9), and accepting God's discipline (chap. 10).

1. Submitting to God's authority (Lev. 8:1-36)

At least twenty times in these three chapters you'll find the word *commanded.* Moses and Aaron didn't have to concoct an ordination ceremony. The same God who instructed Moses how to build the tabernacle also told him how to ordain the priests and how the priests should serve in the tabernacle (Ex. 28–29). Nothing was left to chance or to the imagination. Moses was to do everything according to what God had shown him on the mount (25:40; 26:30; 27:8; Heb. 8:5).

In the ministry of the church today, spiritual leaders must constantly ask, "For what does the Scripture say?" (Rom. 4:3, NKJV) God hasn't left us in the dark as to what His church is, how it's to be led, and what it's supposed to do, but if we substitute people's ideas for God's Word, we *will* be in the dark! (Isa. 8:20) Religious novelties and fads abound, creating celebrities and increasing crowds but not always honoring the Lord or building the church. We need leaders, like Moses, who will spend time "on the mount" and find out from the Word what God wants His people to do.

The assembly called (vv. 1-5). The ordination of Aaron and his sons was a public event as every ordination ought to be (Acts 13:1-3; 16:1-3; 1 Tim. 4:14). First of all the priests would serve God and seek to please Him (Ex. 28:1, 3-4, 41), but also they would be the servants of the people. It would have been impossible for all the people in the camp to assemble at one time at the door of the tabernacle, so it was probably the elders and leaders who gathered, representing the tribes and the various clans (see Lev. 9:1). It's a serious thing to be set apart for ministry, and it must be done under the authority of God and witnessed by God's people.

Aaron and his sons washed (v. 6). This may have been done at the laver in the courtyard of the tabernacle (Ex. 38:8). The priests were ceremonially bathed all over *but once;* from then on, they washed their hands and feet at the laver while they were serving in the tabernacle (30:17-21). When sinners trust Christ, they are washed from their sins once and for all (Rev. 1:5-6; 1 Cor. 6:9-11); God's children need to keep their feet clean by confessing their sins to the Lord (John 13:1-10; 1 John 1:9). In the Bible, water for washing is a picture of the Word of God (Ps. 119:9; John 15:3; Eph. 5:25-27). As we meditate on the Word of God and apply it to our lives, the Spirit of God uses the Word to cleanse us and make us more like Christ (2 Cor. 3:18).

Aaron clothed (vv. 7-9). Aaron and his sons all wore linen undergarments (Ex. 28:42-43; Lev. 6:8-10; see Ex. 20:26), but the high priest wore special beautiful garments, described in Exodus 28. First, Moses put on Aaron the beautifully woven white coat and tied it with the sash. Over that he put the blue robe that had the golden bells and pomegranates on the hem. Over this went the linen ephod, a sleeveless coat that was bound with a special belt; both the ephod and the belt were beautifully embroidered with threads of scarlet, blue, purple, and gold. Over the ephod was the breastplate, an embroidered piece of cloth folded double, on which were twelve precious stones representing the twelve tribes of Israel, and in which were "the Urim and Thummim."[1] On his head, the high priest wore a linen turban (or bonnet) with a special golden "crown" at the front on which were engraved the words HOLY TO THE LORD.

Each "believer priest" has been clothed in the beauty and righteousness of Jesus Christ and is accepted in Him (Isa. 61:10; 2 Cor. 5:21; Eph. 1:6). Our righteousnesses are but filthy rags in God's sight (Isa. 64:6). What must our sins look like to a holy God! The high priest was accepted before God because of the garments God provided in His grace.

Aaron and the tabernacle anointed (vv. 10-12). This was done with a special oil that no one was to duplicate in the camp, nor was it to be used on anyone but a priest (Ex. 30:22-33). In Scripture, oil is often a symbol of the Spirit of God who has anointed each believer (2 Cor. 1:21; 1 John 2:20, 27; see Ps. 133). The Hebrew word "Messiah" and the Greek word "Christ" both mean "anointed one" (Luke 4:18; Acts 10:38). The fact that "the anointing oil of the Lord" was on the priests set them apart from the common people and governed what they could and could not do (Lev. 8:30; 10:7; 21:12, 20).

Aaron's sons clothed (v. 13). They didn't have the beautiful garments of the high priest, but what they wore was still commanded by God; for their linen coats and turbans symbolized holiness before God in character and conduct. "But put on the Lord Jesus Christ, and make no provision for the flesh, to fulfill its lusts" (Rom. 13:14, NKJV).

The various sacrifices offered (vv. 14-29). The bullock for the sin offering for Aaron and his sons made possible the cleansing of their sins, and the ram for the burnt offering symbolized their total dedication to the Lord. The blood of the sin offering even sanctified the altar.

The "ram of consecration [ordination]" took the place of

the fellowship offering, symbolizing their communion with one another and with the Lord. The word translated "consecration" or "ordination" means "to fill up." A part of the sacrifice, along with a meal offering (vv. 25-26), was placed in Aaron's hands, thus filling them up, and then waved before the Lord. Later, this would be eaten. But the unique part of the ceremony was the putting of blood and oil on the right ear, right thumb, and right big toe of Aaron and his sons, symbolizing that they were set apart to hear God's voice, do God's work, and walk in God's ways.

It was necessary that blood be shed before God could accept Aaron and his sons as servants in His holy tabernacle. Because He is the holy Son of God, Jesus Christ our High Priest needed no such sacrifices (Heb. 9). Instead, He is the one perfect sacrifice that "takes away the sin of the world" (John 1:29, NKJV).

The priests anointed (v. 30). Aaron had already had the holy oil poured upon him (Lev. 8:12), but now both he and his sons were sprinkled with both the oil and the blood of the sacrifices, taken from the altar. This meant that both they and their garments were "sanctified," set apart by God for His exclusive use. Neither the priests nor what they wore could be used for any "common" purposes. They belonged wholly to God.

The ordination ram eaten (vv. 31-36). For the next week, Aaron and his sons had to remain in the tabernacle court, and each day, Moses offered sacrifices like those he had offered on "ordination day" (Ex. 29:35-36). The priests then ate the meat of the "ram of ordination" as well as the bread for the meal offering, just as they would have eaten the fellowship offerings. However, there was a difference; they were not permitted to eat the meat the next day (Lev. 7:15-16). Whatever was left over had to be burned that same day. Their seven days in the tabernacle precincts indicated the completion of their dedication to the Lord. Had they disobeyed and left the tabernacle, they would have died. It was a serious thing to be one of God's priests.[2]

2. Revealing God's glory (Lev. 9:1-24)

Aaron and his sons had obeyed God's commandments. Thus when the week was over, they were ready to begin serving the Lord at the altar. Up to this point, Moses had been offering the sacrifices; now Aaron and his sons would take up their priestly ministry.

Sacrificing on God's altar (vv. 1-21). Aaron and his sons had to offer a bull calf for a sin offering and a ram for a burnt offering; from then on, they would be offering a burnt offering on the altar every morning and evening (v. 16; Ex. 29:38-42). Each day must begin and end with total consecration to the Lord. Being imperfect, the priests had to offer sacrifices for themselves first before they could offer sacrifices for the people (see Heb. 7:25-28).

Their ordination, however, also involved offering sacrifices for the people (Lev. 9:3-4): a goat for a sin offering, a calf and a lamb for burnt offerings, and a bullock and a ram for peace (fellowship) offerings, along with the meal offerings. To have sanctified priests without a sanctified people would not be right. How gracious of God to provide for sinners a way of forgiveness, dedication, and fellowship; we have all of this in our Lord Jesus Christ!

Moses spoke to the people and told them that the glory of the Lord would appear when the ordination was completed (v. 6), just as His glory had appeared when the tabernacle was erected (Ex. 40:34-38). *One of the main purposes of the tabernacle ministry was to glorify the God of Israel whose glory dwelt on the mercy seat in the holy of holies.* The pagan nations around them had priests and sacrifices, but they didn't have the glory of God. Instead, they "glorified Him not as God" and "changed the glory of the uncorruptible God into an image" (Rom. 1:21, 23). God hates idolatry because it robs Him of the glory that is due to Him, and it robs God's people of the blessings He wants to share with them.

When Aaron had completed all these sacrifices, he and his sons and the people of Israel were forgiven, dedicated wholly to the Lord and in fellowship with Him. The order of the sacrifices is significant: We must first deal with our sins before we can dedicate ourselves totally to the Lord; then we can enjoy fellowship with Him.

Sharing God's blessing (vv. 22-23a). One of the privileges of the high priest was that of blessing the people; on that first day of his ministry, Aaron gave them *two* blessings. He gave the first one alone, after he had offered the sacrifices; he gave the second one along with Moses after they had come out from the tabernacle when the ordination ceremony was finished.

The first blessing was probably the high priestly blessing recorded in Numbers 6:23-26. It followed the sacrifices. This reminds us that every blessing that we have comes because of the finished work of Jesus Christ on the cross (Eph. 1:3-7). Unless we know Jesus Christ as our own Savior and Lord, we don't have any spiritual blessings of our own, and we can't ask God to bless others through us. The second blessing followed the time Moses and Aaron had in the tabernacle, and this reminds us that we must be in fellowship with God and one another if we're to be a blessing to others.

Seeing God's glory (vv. 23-24). The glory of the Lord had appeared when Moses finished erecting the tabernacle (Ex. 40:34-35), and it would appear again at the dedication of the temple (2 Chron. 7:1ff). How gracious on God's part to share His glory with sinful people!

The glory that dwelt in the tabernacle eventually left the camp because of the sins of the people (1 Sam. 4:21). It returned at the dedication of the temple, but then the Prophet Ezekiel watched it depart because the nation had become so sinful (Ezek. 8:4; 9:3; 10:4, 18; 11:22-23). The glory came to earth when Jesus was born (Luke 2:8-9) and tabernacled in Him (John 1:14), but sinful people nailed that glory to a cross. Today, God's glory dwells in the bodies of His people (1 Cor. 6:19-20), in each local assembly of His people (3:16-17), and in His church collectively (Eph. 2:19-22). One day, we shall see that glory lighting the perfect heavenly city that God is preparing for His people (Rev. 21:22-23).

The fire of God consumed the burnt offering (see 2 Chron. 7:1-3) and gave the people the assurance that Jehovah God was among them and with them. "Our God is a consuming fire" (Heb. 12:29), and that fire could have consumed the people! This reminds us that the wrath of God fell on His Son rather than on sinners who deserved to be judged (2 Cor. 5:21; 1 Peter 2:24).

The paradoxical response of the people helps us better understand the experience of worship, for they were both joyful and overwhelmed. There was joy in their hearts that the true and living God had deigned to dwell among them and receive their worship, but there was also fear as the people fell on their faces in awe. The two attitudes balance each other. "Serve the Lord with fear, and rejoice with trembling" (Ps. 2:11). Paul saw this as a desirable and normal experience in the local assembly (1 Cor. 14:23-25). If our ministry doesn't glorify God, then God can't bless it and use it to help others and win the lost.

3. Accepting God's discipline (Lev. 10:1-20)

A day which should have ended with the glorious worship of Jehovah God was instead climaxed with the funeral of two of Aaron's sons. The words of C.H. Mackintosh are pertinent and powerful:

38

The page of human history has ever been a sadly blotted one. It is a record of failure from first to last. Amid all the delights of Eden, man hearkened to the tempter's lie (Gen. 3); when preserved from judgment by the hand of electing love, and introduced into a restored earth, he was guilty of the sin of intemperance (Gen. 9); when conducted, by Jehovah's outstretched arm, into the land of Canaan, he "forsook the Lord, and served Baal and Ashtaroth" (Judges 2:3); when placed at the very summit of earthly power and glory, with untold wealth at his feet, and all the resources of the world at his command, he gave his heart to the uncircumcised stranger (1 Kings 11). No sooner had the blessings of the gospel been promulgated than it became needful for the Holy Ghost to prophesy concerning "grievous wolves," "apostasy," and all manner of failure. . . . Thus, man spoils everything.[3]

Nadab and Abihu's sin (vv. 1-2). Everything that these two men did was wrong. To begin with, they were *the wrong people* to be handling the incense and presenting it to the Lord. This was the task of their father, the high priest (Ex. 30:7-10). They also used *the wrong instruments,* their own censers instead of the censer of the high priest, sanctified by the special anointing oil (40:9). They acted at *the wrong time,* for it was only on the annual Day of Atonement that the high priest was permitted to take incense into the holy of holies, and even then he had to submit to a special ritual (Lev. 16:1ff).

They acted under *the wrong authority.* They didn't consult with Moses or their father, nor did they seek to follow the Word of God, which Moses had received. In burning the incense, they used *the wrong fire,* what Scripture calls "strange fire" (10:1; NIV says "unauthorized fire"). The high priest was commanded to burn the incense on coals taken from the brazen altar (16:12), but Nadab and Abihu supplied their own fire, and God rejected it. They acted from *the wrong motive* and didn't seek to glorify God alone (10:3). We don't know the secrets of their hearts, but you get the impression that what they did was a willful act of pride. Their desire wasn't to sanctify and glorify the Lord but to promote themselves and be important.

Finally, they depended on *the wrong energy;* for verses 9-10 imply that they were under the influence of alcohol. This reminds us of Ephesians 5:18, "And be not drunk with wine . . . but be filled with the Spirit." If every child of God were killed who substituted fleshly energy for the power of the Spirit, not many would be left! A.W. Tozer once said, "If God were to take His Holy Spirit out of this world, much of what the church is doing would go right on; and nobody would know the difference."

Nadab and Abihu were not outsiders; they were anointed priests *who had seen God on the mountain* (Ex. 24:1-11). Their father was the high priest, and they were trained in the service of the Lord. Yet they were killed for their disobedience! "So, if you think you are standing firm, be careful that you don't fall!" (1 Cor. 10:12, NIV) It's a serious thing to be a servant of God, and our service must be empowered by His Spirit and controlled by His Word. We must serve God "acceptably with reverence and godly fear: for our God is a consuming fire" (Heb. 12:28-29).

Aaron's sorrow (vv. 3-11). With the privileges of ministry come also responsibilities and sacrifices. Aaron wasn't permitted to mourn the death of his two older sons (Lev. 10:6-7; 21:10-12) but had to remain in the tabernacle precincts and complete the ceremony of ordination. Two of his nephews took care of the burial of the bodies (Ex. 6:21-22).

It may seem strange to us that God killed Nadab and Abihu

instead of merely warning them, but often at the beginning of a new era in salvation history, the Lord brought judgment in order to warn the people. The priestly ministry at the tabernacle was about to begin, and the Lord wanted to be sure the priests understood the seriousness of their work. When Israel entered the Promised Land, God used Achan's disobedience as a warning (Josh. 7), and the death of Uzzah was His warning when the ark was brought to Jerusalem (2 Sam. 6:1-7). Early in the Church Age, the death of Ananias and Sapphira served as a warning to the saints not to try to lie to God (Acts 5).

It wasn't enough for the priests merely to teach the people the difference between the holy and the unholy; they also had to practice it in their own lives. This is one of the burdens of the message of Ezekiel the prophet (Ezek. 22:26; 42:20; 44:23; 48:14-15).

Aaron's sincerity (vv. 12-20). Since Moses was concerned lest any other commandment of the Lord be disobeyed and His judgment fall again, he admonished Aaron and his two remaining sons to be sure to eat their share of the peace (fellowship) offerings (Lev. 7:28-36). They were also to eat their part of the sin offering (6:24-30). Moses discovered that the sin offering hadn't been presented according to the law and that Aaron and his sons hadn't eaten it. At first he was angry, but Aaron's explanation satisfied him.

Aaron explained that he couldn't eat the offering with a good conscience because of the sorrow that had befallen him that day. The Lord knew his heart, and he wasn't going to attempt to fool God by playing the hypocrite. Aaron knew that a mere mechanical observance of the ritual wouldn't have pleased God; for the Lord looks on the heart and wants obedience, not sacrifice (1 Sam. 15:22-23; 16:7; Ps. 51:16-17; Micah 6:6-8). The law didn't allow Aaron to express his grief in the usual ways, but it didn't forbid him to fast; and fasting was his way of showing his grief for the loss of his two sons.

As you review these three chapters, several lessons stand out clearly:

1. God's Word commands us concerning our ministry, and we must obey what He says. God's instructions are more detailed for the Old Testament priests than for New Testament ministers, but the principles and examples are clearly given in the New Testament so that we shouldn't go astray.

2. We dedicate ourselves to God, and He consecrates us for His service. He wants servants who are clean, yielded, obedient, and "marked" by the blood and the oil.

3. Apart from the finished work of Christ and the power of the Spirit, we can't serve God acceptably (1 Peter 2:5). No amount of fleshly zeal or "false fire" can substitute for Spirit-filled devotion to the Lord. Be sure the "fire" of your ministry comes from God's altar and not from this world.

4. We minister first of all to the Lord and for His glory. No matter how much we sacrifice and serve, if God doesn't get the glory, there can be no blessing.

5. The privileges of ministry bring with them serious responsibilities. "For everyone to whom much is given, from him much will be required" (Luke 12:48, NKJV).

6. Our greatest joy in life should be to serve the Lord and bring glory to His name. "Serve the Lord with fear, and rejoice with trembling" (Ps. 2:11, NKJV).

F O U R

Cleanliness and Godliness

"Cleanliness is next to godliness."

John Wesley is generally credited with that saying;[1] but it's likely the proverb was current before his time. In fact, the way Wesley quoted it in his sermon "On Dress" indicates that his listeners were already familiar with the maxim.

The Jews would readily identify with the saying; in the camp of Israel, the concepts of *cleanliness* and *godliness* were so intertwined that they were almost synonymous. The Jews feared lest they become ceremonially unclean because of something they had touched or eaten. From birth to burial, the Jews had to submit every aspect of their daily lives to the authority of God's law. Whether it was selecting their food, preparing their food, caring for a mother and new baby, diagnosing a disease, or disposing of waste, nothing was left to chance in the camp of Israel lest someone be defiled. In order to maintain ceremonial purity, each Jew had to obey God's law in several areas of life.

1. Eating (Lev. 11:1-23)
Since Noah knew about clean and unclean animals (Gen. 7:1-10), this distinction was part of an ancient tradition that ante-

dated the Mosaic Law. Whether a creature was "clean" or "unclean" had nothing to do with the quality of the beast; it all depended on what God said about the animal. When He gave these laws, no doubt the Lord had the health of His people in mind (Ex. 15:26; Deut. 7:15), but the main purpose of the dietary code was to remind the Israelites that they belonged to God and were obligated to keep themselves separated from everything that would defile them. "Be holy, for I am holy" (Lev. 11:44; see Deuteronomy 14:3-20 for a parallel list of clean and unclean foods).

Nevertheless, the spiritual principle of separation from defilement applies to the people of God today. The fact that we know God must make a difference in every aspect of our lives. "For you were bought at a price; therefore glorify God in your body and in your spirit, which are God's" (1 Cor. 6:20, NKJV). "Therefore, whether you eat or drink, or whatever you do, do all to the glory of God" (10:31, NKJV). God hasn't given His church a list of things that are clean and unclean, but He's revealed enough to us in His Word to help us know what pleases Him and what grieves Him.

Three facts should be noted about the dietary laws: (1) God gave these laws only to the Jewish nation; (2) obeying them guaranteed ceremonial purity but didn't automatically make the person holy in character; and (3) the laws were temporary and were ended on the cross of Christ (Col. 2:14).

Jesus made it clear to His disciples that all foods were clean (Mark 7:1ff), and God taught this lesson again to Peter before He sent him to minister to the "unclean" Gentiles (Acts 10:9-16). Paul affirmed that special days and diets must not be considered either the *means* or the *measure* of a person's spirituality (Rom. 14:1–15:13). "But food does not bring us near to God; we are no worse if we do not eat, and no better if we do" (1 Cor. 8:8, NIV). It's wrong to judge other Christians on the basis of what they eat (Col. 2:16-23). As long as they believe God's Word that all foods are clean, and ask God to bless their food, they have the right to eat it (1 Tim. 4:1-6).[2]

It isn't necessary to identify every creature named in this chapter. In fact, some of them are mysteries to us. Keep in mind that the law named *representative* creatures and didn't attempt to give a complete list. Moses gave the general characteristics of the creatures that were approved and disapproved, and the people had to exercise discernment in applying the law. If a creature was doubtful, it was rejected; there was no sense taking a chance of becoming defiled.

Land animals (vv. 1-8). The two requirements were that the animal chew the cud and have a split hoof. An animal with only one of these features wasn't considered clean and had to be rejected. The Hebrew word translated "hare" in verse 6 ("rabbit," NIV) refers to an animal we're not familiar with, because the kinds of rabbits we're familiar with don't chew the cud. The movements of a rabbit's jaw and nostrils may give the appearance that he's chewing the cud, but that isn't the case at all.

Water creatures (vv. 9-12). These had to have both fins and scales to be edible; and so all shellfish, catfish, and eels were prohibited. Aquatic creatures that are scavengers and burrow in the bottom of a body of water could pick up parasites that would be dangerous to the eater's health. Since fish swim freely in the water, they generally escape such infections.

Fowl (vv. 13-19). Carrion-eating birds of prey would be defiled by the dead carcasses of their victims as well as by the blood still in the flesh; this made them doubly unclean. When Israel lusted after meat, the Lord sent them quails (Ex. 16:1-13; Num. 11:31-35).

Flying insects (vv. 20-23). All insects were forbidden except those with jointed hind legs used for jumping, such as locusts, katydids, crickets, and grasshoppers. These creatures aren't normally a part of the Western diet, but many peoples in the East eat parts of their bodies roasted. John the Baptist lived on a diet of locusts and wild honey (Matt. 3:4). The Jews would shun cockroaches, flies, and other insects of that variety.

Some years ago, during the course of my annual physical examination, my doctor discovered that my sugar count was rather high. He checked it very carefully and then informed me that I was a borderline diabetic in danger of experiencing some serious calamity, like a heart attack or blindness. The easiest solution to my problem was to lose weight, so I immediately went on a diet.

He gave me a piece of good advice. "Remember the secret of a happy diet is to learn to hate the things that aren't good for you and to enjoy the things that are good for you."

It worked! I followed the diet, lost my taste for sweets and rich desserts, and soon got rid of the excess weight that was threatening my health, if not my life. We got the sugar under control.

The Jews under the Old Covenant had to adopt a similar outlook on life. They had to learn to despise the foods that God said were unclean and to enjoy the foods that God said were clean. It was a choice between pleasing themselves and being unclean or pleasing the Lord and being clean. There was no middle ground. If any food was questionable, it should have been automatically rejected, lest they disobey God and defile themselves.

When I was a young believer, somebody gave me a copy of the tract "Others May, You Cannot"; it was a big help to me. I learned that I had to get my directions from God and not from other people, and that I had to be willing to be different. My great desire had to be to please the Lord joyfully, not grudgingly, and not to see how close I could get to sin and still not get into trouble.

2. Touching (Lev. 11:24-43)

The emphasis in this section is on avoiding the defilement caused by touching certain dead creatures, both clean and unclean. If a Jew happened upon the carcass of even a clean animal, he knew it was defiled because the blood hadn't been properly drained out nor had the meat been protected from contamination. When Samson ate the honey from the carcass of the lion, he defiled himself and ceased to be a Nazarite (Jud. 14:1-9; see Num. 6:6, 9). No matter how sweet the honey was, it was unclean in God's sight; this made Samson unclean.

People who became defiled from touching a carcass were considered unclean until the end of the day. They had to wash themselves and their clothes and couldn't enter the camp until sunset. This kept them from spreading to others any contamination they might have picked up from touching the dead animal. If a dead creature fell into an earthen vessel, the vessel was smashed. Anything touched by the carcass was unclean and had to be either washed or destroyed.

It's easy to see hygienic reasons behind these regulations, and no doubt obeying them helped the Jews avoid sickness. But the main reason for these laws was to teach the people to appreciate cleanliness and shun whatever was unclean. Paul's admonition of the Corinthians is a contemporary application of this principle and must be pondered and obeyed by any believer who is serious about holy living (2 Cor. 6:14–7:1).

Moses also added lizards, rodents, and other creeping things to the list of prohibited foods (Lev. 11:29-30). These small creatures could die and be so concealed that a person would not know the carcass was there before they had touched it and become defiled. Or the corpse might fall into a container or on fabric, and this would make the item unclean. Jewish women were very careful in their housekeeping lest anything be present that would make the inhabitants unclean.

Thirty-two times in Leviticus 11, you find the word *unclean,* and ten times you find the word *abomination.* What God says is unclean must be an abomination in our eyes. "Woe to those who call evil good and good evil, who put darkness for light and light for darkness" (Isa. 5:20, NIV). The first step toward disobedience is often "reclassifying" sin and making it look acceptable instead of abominable.

For example, God said that the tree in the midst of the garden was off-limits to the man and woman, but Eve "saw that the tree was good for food" (Gen. 3:6) and took the fruit. God said that all the spoil of Jericho was under divine restriction and not to be touched by the Jewish soldiers (Josh. 6:16-19), but Achan revised that classification and took some of the spoil (7:16-26). It cost him his life. Samuel told King Saul to slay all the Amalekites and their flocks and herds, but the king kept Agag alive and kept "the best of the sheep and of the oxen" to give to the Lord (1 Sam. 15:15). Saul reclassified what God had said was abominable and thought this would make it acceptable, but his folly caused him to lose his kingdom.

Today, we live in a society that rejects moral absolutes and promotes a "fluid" morality that isn't morality at all. Like the people described in the Book of Judges, everybody is doing what is right in their own eyes (Jud. 21:25). But society's reclassifying of sin hasn't changed anything; God still calls sin an abomination and still judges it.

Doctors can be sued for malpractice if they make the wrong diagnosis and prescribe the wrong treatment. But a university professor, a liberal preacher, or a popular newspaper columnist can excuse sin and defend immorality and be applauded for the skillful diagnosis. Why? Because the human heart is "deceitful above all things, and desperately wicked" (Jer. 17:9) and people love "darkness rather than light" because their deeds are evil (John 3:19).

Evangelist Billy Sunday used to say that a sinner can't find God for the same reason a criminal can't find a police officer: the criminal isn't looking very hard! "Prophets and priests alike, all practice deceit," wrote Jeremiah the prophet. "They dress the wound of My people as though it were not serious. 'Peace, peace,' they say, when there is no peace" (Jer. 8:11, NIV). The people are persecuted who have the right diagnosis and the only remedy, while the people with the false diagnosis and the useless remedy are honored. "The prophets prophesy falsely, and the priests bear rule by their means; and My people love to have it so" (5:31).

3. Discerning (Lev. 11:44-47)

If the Jewish people were to keep themselves clean and pleasing to the Lord, they had to exercise discernment; this meant knowing God's Word, respecting it, and obeying it. Fathers and mothers had to teach their children the law and warn them about the things that were unclean (Deut. 6:1-9). The priests had to teach the people and remind them of the commandments of the Lord. It was when the nation of Israel neglected the Word of God and refused to obey it that the people began to follow the abominable practices of the heathen nations around them, and this is what led to Israel's discipline and defeat.

The Jews had to remind themselves every hour of every day that they belonged to Jehovah, the true and living God, and that belonging to the nation of Israel was a high and holy privilege. "I am the Lord your God; consecrate yourselves and be holy, because I am holy" (Lev. 11:44, NIV). In New Testament language, "Walk worthy of the calling with which you were called" (Eph. 4:1, NKJV). Obeying God's will isn't a burden; it's a privilege! As Moses reminded his people, "For what great nation is there that has God so near to it, as the Lord our God is to us, for whatever reason we may call upon

Him? And what great nation is there that has such statutes and righteous judgments as are in all this law which I set before you this day?" (Deut. 4:7-8, NKJV)

The Old Testament Jew, like the New Testament Christian, was not to walk "as other Gentiles walk, in the vanity of their mind" (Eph. 4:17). It was a temptation to "go along with" and then imitate the pagan practices of the heathen nations, and this led to Israel's defilement and discipline. I fear that the church today is following the same philosophy and becoming more and more like the world. G. Campbell Morgan was right when he said that the church did the most for the world when the church was the least like the world.

Jews who exercised spiritual discernment would "walk in love" (Eph. 5:2), and their love for the Lord would motivate them to obey His law. Each morning, the orthodox Jew would recite "The Shema," the official Jewish confession of faith: "Hear, O Israel: The Lord our God, the Lord is one. Love the Lord your God with all your heart and with all your soul and with all your strength" (Deut. 6:4-5, NIV). That is still the first great commandment (Matt. 22:34-40).

Like Israel in the Old Testament, believers today must not only walk worthy of their calling and walk in love, but also must "walk circumspectly . . . understanding what the will of the Lord is" (Eph. 5:15, 17). We must keep our eyes open and look around carefully lest we defile ourselves. Jews who knew what God said was clean and unclean, and who exercised constant caution, weren't likely to touch something unclean and defile themselves. When we "walk as children of light" (Eph. 5:8), we won't stumble over some carcass in the darkness; for God's Word is the light that directs us (Ps. 119:105).

The Lord reminded His people that it was He who had redeemed them from Egyptian bondage (Lev. 11:45). Therefore, they belonged to Him and were obligated to obey His will. Christ has redeemed us, not that we might be free to please ourselves, but that we might be free to serve Him, which is the greatest freedom of all. In giving His law, the Lord frequently used the miracle of the Exodus to call Israel to obedience (19:36; 22:31-33; 25:38, 42, 55; 26:13, 45). In New Testament language, the Jews had been "bought with a price" and were obligated to glorify the Lord who had redeemed them (1 Cor. 6:20; 1 Peter 1:18-25).

One of the marks of maturity is the ability "to make a difference" (Lev. 11:47) and distinguish between right and wrong. As a pathologist looks through his or her microscope, he or she can see a difference between a healthy cell and a cancerous cell. The expert musician can hear the difference between the right note and the almost-right note, and the expert writer knows the difference between "any word" and the right word. Likewise, mature believers can exercise discernment, identify that which is unclean, and avoid it. Remember, children are prone to walk into the mud and get dirty.

What the Prophet Hosea said about Israel in his day is true of many professed Christians today: "You stumble day and night, and the prophets stumble with you . . . My people are destroyed from lack of knowledge" (Hosea 4:5-6, NIV). "But solid food is for the mature, who by constant use have trained themselves to distinguish good from evil" (Heb. 5:14, NIV). Commenting on 1 Corinthians 2:13-16, Vance Havner said, "Nothing is more rare in churches today than discernment. The natural man knows nothing of it, the carnal man is devoid of it. Only the spiritual man has it and we have all too few in that category."

4. Purifying (Lev. 12:1-8)
God graciously made provision for the cleansing and restoration of anyone who became defiled. For routine situations of

uncleanness, the normal procedure was for people to wash themselves and their clothing and remain outside the camp until evening. Numbers 19 describes the preparation of special "water of purification" that was kept outside the camp and used for ceremonial cleansing. But with some kinds of defilement, additional measures were necessary, as in cases of childbirth (Lev. 12) and the presence of infectious sores or diseases (chaps. 13–15).

Mother and child (vv. 1-5). In giving birth to a baby, the mother experienced bleeding (vv. 4-5, 7), as well as the secretion of other bodily fluids (see chap. 15); and this made her *ceremonially* unclean. The theme of this chapter is not personal holiness but *ritual* purification for the mother, without which she could not return to normal life in her home and in the camp.

Therefore, nothing in Leviticus 12 should be interpreted to teach that human sexuality is "dirty," that pregnancy is defiling, or that babies are impure. God created humans "male and female" (Gen. 1:27), and when God declared His creation to be "very good" (v. 31), that declaration included sex. He commanded our first parents to "be fruitful, and multiply" (v. 28); in spite of contemporary negative attitudes toward babies, Scripture presents children as blessings from God (Pss. 113:9; 127:3-5; 128:3; Prov. 17:6; Matt. 19:14). If for some reason a pregnancy was unwanted, the Jews would never consider aborting the baby.

There are probably matters of health involved in these instructions. Since the mother was considered to some measure "unclean" for forty days after the birth of a son, or eighty days after the birth of a daughter, it meant that she had opportunity for rest and recuperation before returning to her household duties. This would encourage her own well-being as well as that of the baby. It would also protect her from possible sickness carried by infected people seeking to assist her, or the spread of any infection she might have (that is, childbed fever).

Scripture doesn't explain why twice as much time is assigned to a daughter than to a son. There's no proof that girl babies are necessarily weaker than boy babies and therefore need a longer time with the mother. A daughter would one day be subject to the judgment placed on Eve (Gen. 3:16), but why would God double the confinement of the mother because of the sex of her child, something over which she had no control? And it doesn't seem reasonable that God set up this schedule in order to "punish" the husband by doubling the time he'd have to be apart from his wife. Perhaps God established these regulations primarily for the health of the mother and her "bonding" to her daughter. The social structure of Israel was decidedly masculine, and sons were more welcome than daughters.

Circumcision (v. 3).[4] In ancient days, other nations practiced circumcision; but God gave this rite to Abraham as a special mark of the covenant He had with the people of Israel (Gen. 17:10-14). Each male child became a "child of the covenant" when he was circumcised and named eight days after his birth. The operation also symbolized the "spiritual surgery" that God wants to perform on the human heart (Deut. 10:16; 30:6; Jer. 4:4). Unfortunately, the Jewish people ignored the spiritual aspect of the ceremony and considered the physical operation alone a guarantee that the Jews were saved and accepted by God (Matt. 3:7-10; Rom. 2:25-29). A similar idea emerged in the early church and had to be strongly refuted (Acts 15; Rom. 4:1-12).

Some people equate infant baptism with circumcision; but as R.K. Harrison wisely states it, "The parallels are too superficial and narrow to be entirely convincing or valid."[4] The true believer has experienced an inner spiritual circumcision through the Holy Spirit, the "true circumcision" that changes the heart and imparts new life (Gal. 6:12-16; Phil. 3:1-3; Col. 2:10-11). Because the sinful nature of the believer has been "put off," he or she can walk in newness of life and does not have to yield to the desires of the flesh.

Sacrifice (vv. 4-8). Forty days after the birth of a son, or eighty days after the birth of a daughter, the mother and father were required to go to the sanctuary and offer the sacrifices for the mother's cleansing; a year-old lamb for a burnt offering and a dove or pigeon for a sin offering. The burnt offering symbolized her dedication to God as she returned to her normal life, and the sin offering took care of the defilement involved in the birth process. It also reminded them that every child, no matter how beautiful or delightful he or she might be, is born in sin and must one day trust the Lord for salvation (Pss. 51:5; 58:3).

How gracious of God to make allowances for the poor who couldn't afford a lamb! Mary and Joseph took advantage of this provision when they brought Jesus to the temple (Luke 2:21-24).

This entire chapter, brief as it is, shows God's loving concern for the family, especially mother and child. We aren't at all surprised to hear Jesus say, "Let the little children come to Me, and do not hinder them, for the kingdom of God belongs to such as these" (Mark 10:14, NIV).

The Great Physician

The beginning of health is to know the disease," wrote the Spanish novelist Miguel de Cervantes, and every physician would agree with him. After all, how can you prescribe effectively if you don't diagnose accurately?

These three chapters in Leviticus deal with bodily infirmities of one kind or another, because God was concerned about His people's physical welfare. He cared for their needs during their wilderness march (Deut. 29:5) and, if they obeyed Him, He promised to shield them from the diseases they'd seen in Egypt (Ex. 15:26; Deut. 7:12-15). While it's true that our greatest needs are spiritual, God still has the physical well-being of His people at heart.

The Hebrew word translated *leprosy* in Leviticus 14–15 includes various skin diseases and even mildew (13:47ff; 14:33ff). But there's more to these chapters than simply a description of symptoms and ceremonies. In Scripture, disease is one of the images of sin (Ps. 147:3; Isa. 1:5-6; Jer. 8:2; 30:12; Mark 2:17). Thus as we study these chapters, we can learn what sin is like and how God wants us to deal with it. We must look beyond Moses to Jesus Christ, the Great Physician, who was wounded that we might be healed (Isa. 53:5).

These three chapters illustrate three topics that are vitally related to the life of holiness: sin (Lev. 13), salvation (chap. 14), and sanctity (chap. 15).

1. Sin (Lev. 13:1-46; 14:1-32)

Since infection made a person ceremonially unclean, God appointed the priests to act as His examiners to determine whether the victim was "unclean" and therefore had to be separated from the rest of the camp. The person being examined could be isolated for as long as two weeks to give the disease a chance to change for better or for worse. The symptoms might involve swelling and a rash (13:1-8); swelling, whiteness, and raw flesh (vv. 9-17); boils (vv. 18-23); burns (vv. 24-28); and various skin eruptions (vv. 29-44). Not everything that looked like leprosy actually was leprosy, and it would be cruel to isolate somebody who wasn't actually infected.

Note also that the investigation included not only persons (vv. 1-46), but also clothing (vv. 47-59) and even houses (14:33-57). Here the priest was looking for a mildew or fungus that, if allowed to spread, could do serious damage. Once Israel was in their land, these fungi could even destroy their crops (Deut. 28:22; Amos 4:9).

Since disease is an illustration of sin in the Bible, as you read these verses, you will learn a great deal about the "symptoms" of sin.

Sin is "deeper than the skin" (13:3-4, 25, 30-32, 34). "The heart is deceitful above all things, and desperately wicked: who can know it?" (Jer. 17:9) The word translated "wicked" in this verse means "sick"; the NIV translates it "beyond cure." Sin is not a surface problem that can be solved with simple remedies, like trying to cure cancer with hand lotion. Sin comes from within, from fallen human nature; unless the heart is changed, there can be no solving of the sin problem.

"For I know that in me (that is, in my flesh) nothing good dwells" (Rom. 7:18, NKJV). Those who talk about the "innate goodness of man" know neither the Bible nor their own hearts.

In eighteenth-century England, if you were convicted for stealing, the judge could order the authorities to chop off your right hand. If you were convicted a second time, they could cut off the left hand. I recall reading about a pickpocket who lost both hands but managed to succeed in his career because he perfected picking pockets *with his teeth!* Even if the authorities had pulled all his teeth, it wouldn't have solved the problem, because sin is deeper than the skin. Jesus said, "For out of the heart proceed evil thoughts, murders, adulteries, fornications, thefts, false witness, blasphemies: These are the things which defile a man" (Matt. 15:19-20).

In Jeremiah's day, the false prophets were like physicians who lied to their patients and refused to give them bad news. "They have healed also the hurt of the daughter of My people slightly, saying, Peace, peace; when there is no peace" (Jer. 6:14). The medical profession today would discipline a doctor who did that, but the practice is perfectly acceptable for humanistic counselors, liberal preachers and professors, politicians, and newspaper columnists. People still believe the "progress myth" that people are good and are making themselves and the world better and better day by day.

Sin spreads (13:5-8, 22-23, 27-28, 32, 34-36, 51, 53, 55, 57; 14:39, 44, 48). True leprosy ("Hansen's disease") affects the skin and the nerve endings; as it spreads, it produces nodules and ulcers. The tissues then contract and the limbs become deformed. What begins as one sore gradually spreads and turns the whole body into a mass of corruption and ugliness. How like sin! "Then, when desire has conceived, it gives birth to sin; and sin, when it is full-grown, brings forth death" (James 1:15, NKJV).

Our first parents were thieves. Their son Cain was a liar and a murderer. From that small beginning, sin spread so as to corrupt and enslave the whole human race. By the time God sent the Flood, the earth was *filled* with wickedness, evil, violence, and corruption (Gen. 6:5, 11-13); and things haven't become any better since then. Scientific progress has made life more comfortable, but it hasn't made the world less corrupt. "The whole head is sick, and the whole heart faints. From the sole of the foot even to the head, there is no soundness in it, but wounds and bruises and putrefying sores" (Isa. 1:5-6, NKJV).

For nearly fifty years, Alexander Whyte preached God's Word at Free St. George's Church in Edinburgh, Scotland, and gained a reputation for exposing the sins of the human heart and bringing them under the scrutiny of the Word of God. "Surgical preaching" people called it. At one time, he had an assistant named Hugh Black who preached at the evening service and was much more liberal and optimistic in his message. The congregation said they were blackened by Whyte on Sunday mornings and whitewashed by Black on Sunday evenings!

But when the church has a superficial view of sin, this attitude affects everything the church believes and does. If men and women are basically good and not sinners under the wrath of God, then why preach the Gospel? Why send out missionaries? For that matter, why did Jesus even die on the cross? If people are good, then what they need is counseling and consoling, not convicting; we should give them encouragement, not evangelism.

Sin defiles (vv. 44-46). The word "unclean" is used fifty-four times in Leviticus 13–15. It describes the ceremonial defilement that makes the victim unfit for social life or for participation in worship at the house of God. The Prophet Isaiah confessed that he was "a man of unclean lips" (Isa.

6:5), and then he spoke for all of us when he wrote, "But we are all as an unclean thing, and all our righteousnesses are as filthy rags" (64:6). Whatever sin touches, it defiles; only the blood of Jesus Christ can wash away that defilement (1 Cor. 6:9-11; 1 John 1:7; Rev. 1:5).

When you read Psalm 51, David's prayer of confession, you can't help but notice how his sins defiled every part of his being: his eyes (v. 3), his mind (v. 6), his ears (v. 8), his bones (v. 8), his heart (v. 10), and his mouth (vv. 13-15). His hands were stained with Uriah's blood (v. 14), and all he could do was throw himself on the mercy of God and cry out, "Wash me!" (vv. 2. 7)

Sin isolates (v. 46). What solemn words: "He is unclean: he shall dwell alone; without the camp shall his habitation be." He had to tear his clothes, put a covering on his upper lip, cry "Unclean, unclean!" whenever anybody approached him, and remain outside the camp until either he died or was healed. "Free among the dead" is the way Heman described it in Psalm 88:5. God struck King Azariah (Uzziah) with leprosy, and he had to dwell in a "separate house," literally "a free house," which was isolated from everybody else (2 Kings 15:5, NIV). He was free—among the dead!

If you've done any witnessing, you've probably met people who seem to have no concept of the tragedy of sin and the awfulness of hell. "I don't mind going to hell," they say rather flippantly. "I'll have lots of company."[1] But there is no company in hell, because hell is a place of eternal isolation and loneliness. Like the lepers outside the camp, lost sinners will dwell alone; they will be alone forever.

Sin is fit only for the fire (vv. 52, 55, 57). A defiled garment was to be burned in the fire; it was not to be purified but destroyed. When Jesus spoke about hell, He used the word *gehenna,* which referred to the garbage dump outside Jerusalem "where their worm dieth not, and the fire is not quenched" (Mark 9:44; see Isa. 66:24). Hell is God's eternal garbage dump prepared for the devil and his angels (Matt. 25:41) *and for those who follow the devil by rejecting Jesus Christ.* It's a lake of fire (Rev. 19:20; 21:10, 14-15) where Satan and his associates will suffer forever along with people whose names were not found in the Book of Life because they hadn't trusted Jesus Christ and been born again into God's family.

The consequences of leprosy were temporal, but the consequences of sin are eternal. The Jews knew no cure for leprosy, but there is a remedy for sin — faith in Jesus Christ, the Savior of the world. Have you trusted Him? If you have, are you telling others the good news that they don't have to be lepers and live forever in the fiery garbage dump of hell?

2. Salvation (Lev. 14:1-32)

I find it discouraging to read chapter 13, with its emphasis on uncleanness and isolation. But chapter 14 brings us that happy ray of hope that we need: A leper can be cleansed and restored! We need the bad news of judgment before we can appreciate the good news of salvation.

The Jews had no cure for leprosy. Thus, if the victim became well, it was a gift of God's mercy and grace. "And many lepers were in Israel in the time of Elisha the prophet," said Jesus, "and none of them was cleansed, saving Naaman the Syrian" (Luke 4:27). "Salvation is of the Lord" (Jonah 2:9). If we aren't saved by God's grace, then we aren't saved at all; for nobody deserves to be saved.

The steps in the leper's cleansing and restoration picture to us what Jesus Christ has done for sinners.

The priest goes to the leper (vv. 1-3). Since the unclean leper wasn't permitted to enter the camp, the priest had to go outside the camp to minister to him or her. "For the Son of man is come to seek and to save that which was lost" (Luke

19:10). When He ministered here on earth, Jesus was called "a friend of publicans and sinners" (Luke 7:34); He compared Himself to a doctor helping his needy patients (Matt. 9:10-13). As God's Great Physician, Jesus makes "house calls" and comes to sinners right where they are. In the case of the Jewish leper, the priest went out to investigate and determine if indeed the victim was healed; but Jesus comes to us that He might heal us of the sickness of sin.

The victim offers the two birds (vv. 4-7). This unusual ritual pictures to us what Christ did to save a lost world. Birds don't belong in clay jars; they belong in the heavens. Jesus came down from heaven and became a man (John 3:13, 31; 6:38, 42). As it were, He put Himself into a clay jar so that He might die for our sins. The running water over which the bird was killed reminds us of the Holy Spirit of God (John 7:37-39), for Jesus offered Himself to God "through the eternal Spirit" (Heb. 9:14). When the blood-stained living bird was turned loose, it pictured our Lord's resurrection; for the resurrection of Christ is as much a part of the Gospel message as is His death (1 Cor. 15:1-4). Only a living Savior can save dead sinners.

The blood of the bird that was sacrificed was in the jar and on the living bird, but it also had to be applied to the healed leper. Using the hyssop (Ex. 12:22; Ps. 51:7), the priest sprinkled the blood on the leper seven times and then pronounced the leper clean.[2] "Without shedding of blood is no remission" (Heb. 9:22). How did the victim know he was clean? The priest told him so! How do believers today know that God has saved us? He tells us so in His Word! No matter how the leper felt or what he looked like, God said he was clean, and that settled it.

The person cleanses himself (vv. 8-9). On the day of his cleansing, he had to wash himself and his garments and shave off all his hair. He was then permitted to enter the camp, but he wasn't allowed to enter his tent. He had to stay outside for another week.

Why wash when the priest had already pronounced him clean? Because he had to apply *personally* what God said was true *positionally*. The man was ceremonially clean and had the *right* to live in the camp, but he needed to be made personally and practically clean so he would be *fit* to live in the camp. "Wash yourselves, make yourselves clean" (Isa. 1:17, NKJV). "Let us cleanse ourselves from all filthiness of the flesh and spirit, perfecting holiness in the fear of God" (2 Cor. 7:1). Perhaps Paul had Leviticus 14 in mind when he compared the new life in Christ to a change of clothes (Col. 3:1-14).

The person cleanses himself again (v. 9). This takes place a week later. The man had to wash, shave his body again, and put on clean clothes. The dual shaving left his skin like that of a baby, perhaps symbolizing a new birth. The shaving and washing didn't kill the germs of leprosy—God had done that—but they symbolized the newness of life that had come to the former leper.

The person offered the required sacrifices (vv. 10-32). It's now the eighth day since the priest first visited the leper, and eight is the number of the new beginning. The cleansed leper must bring to the door of the tabernacle a male lamb for a trespass (guilt) offering, a male lamb for a burnt offering, a ewe lamb for a sin offering, as well as fine flour and oil for a meal offering.

On the basis of these sacrifices, the priest had pronounced the man clean (Lev. 14:7), because these sacrifices picture the person and work of Jesus Christ. The sin offering shows Christ atoning for a person's sin. The trespass offering reminds us that Christ paid the debt we owed to God because, like the leper, we were unable to serve Him during our days of uncleanness. In the burnt offering, the man dedicated himself completely to God, and the meal offering displayed the perfections of Christ accepted for the imperfections of the worshiper.

The unique thing about this ceremony is that *the priest treated the cleansed leper like a fellow priest!* He put the blood of the trespass offering on the man's right ear, right thumb, and right big toe. He sprinkled oil on the man seven times and then put the oil on the blood that was already on his ear, thumb, and toe.[3] After that, he poured the oil on the man's head. This is similar to the ceremony Moses used when he ordained Aaron and his sons (chap. 8).[4] What grace that God should treat a former leper like a priest! Six times in this section the Lord declares that the priest "made atonement" for the man (14:18-21, 29-31), which means that his sins were forgiven.

Since the leper had been an outcast, unable to work and earn money, perhaps he wasn't able to bring all three animals for sacrifices. Thus God permitted the poorer man to bring birds for the sin offering and the burnt offering (vv. 21-23, 30-31). In addition, the Lord didn't require any restitution along with the trespass offering. God makes it as easy as possible for sinners to be forgiven and restored. But sinners act as if salvation is so difficult, that they can't possibly respond to God's call.

3. Sanctity (Lev. 15:1-33)

The key word in this chapter is "issue," used twenty-four times. It simply means a flow of liquid, whether water in nature or a fluid discharged from the human body. The human discharge may be natural (vv. 16-18, 25-30) or unnatural (vv. 1-15, 19-24), but it's still considered unclean and must be dealt with according to the law of God. Personal hygiene and God's concern for women are certainly involved in these regulations, but the main thrust seems to be that of enforcing personal sanctity. Not everybody is a leper, but all of us have occasional "discharges" that defile us and could defile others.

Unnatural male discharges (vv. 1-15). These could be anything from diarrhea to discharges caused by a venereal disease such as gonorrhea. Anything the afflicted man touched or spat upon was unclean. In fact, those defiled by touching him had to wash themselves and their clothes, and they remained unclean until evening. Clay vessels that he touched were to be broken and wooden vessels washed. The possibility of infection was taken very seriously.

By the goodness of the Lord, the man with a discharge could get well; when that happened, he had to wait a week and, like the cleansed leper, wash himself and his clothes. On the eighth day, he brought a sin offering and a burnt offering, but he wasn't required to bring expensive sacrifices, since a bodily discharge wasn't as serious as leprosy. After that, the man was free to worship the Lord and live a normal life in the camp.

In recent years, we've heard a good deal about "toxic people" and even "toxic churches." Stephen Arteburn and Jack Felton have written a book called *Toxic Faith* (Oliver/Nelson, 1991) that describes "cultic" churches and the religious addiction they quietly spread among unsuspecting people. The image is a biblical one, for Jesus warned about people like the Pharisees who pretended to be holy but were really transmitting defilement to the people who followed them (Matt. 23:25-28). In fact, Paul wrote about people in his own day whose religion was "toxic." "Avoid godless chatter, because those who indulge in it will become more and more ungodly. Their teaching will spread like gangrene" (2 Tim. 2:16-17, NIV).

Natural male discharges (vv. 16-18). This paragraph doesn't even suggest that sexual intercourse within marriage is impure or defiling. As the traditional marriage ceremony puts it,

"God established marriage for the blessing and benefit of mankind." Within the holy and loving bonds of marriage, the husband doesn't defile his wife nor the wife her husband. "Marriage should be honored by all, and the marriage bed kept pure, for God will judge the adulterer and all the sexually immoral" (Heb. 13:4, NIV).

Moses is dealing here with *ceremonial* uncleanness, not moral uncleanness. Since intercourse involves bodily fluids, and bodily fluids made a person unclean, the husband and wife had to take pains to wash themselves and maintain ceremonial purity. Perhaps the Lord is telling us that, even in a beautiful experience like married love, there is opportunity for our sinful nature to go to work and defile it. The Jewish couple had to consider God as well as their own desires, and this helped sanctify their relationship. No sacrifices were required for their cleansing, only washing in water. Thus there was no sin that needed to be atoned for.[5]

Natural female discharges (vv. 19-24). Once again, God wasn't condemning or punishing the woman for experiencing her normal monthly period, because He made her that way so she could bear children. This regulation declares only that the woman's discharge made her unclean and therefore she could make others unclean. Rachel used this ploy when she deceived her father about his household gods (Gen. 31:26-35).

During the time of her period and for a week afterward, a woman was unclean and had to be careful where she sat and slept and what she touched. But this confinement was a blessing in disguise since it allowed her to enjoy rest and quiet when she needed it most. If her husband was too aggressive sexually, this law kept him from taking advantage of her at a time when intercourse wouldn't be especially pleasant to her. If he forced himself on her, both he and the marriage bed would be unclean for a week, and this would separate him from everybody in the family and the camp! It wasn't worth it.[6]

Certainly God created sex for pleasure as well as for procreation, but pleasure that isn't disciplined soon becomes bondage and then torture. Unmarried people must exercise self-control lest they commit fornication and invite the judgment of God (Heb. 13:4), but married people also need self-control lest they take advantage of one another and leave God out of their most intimate relationship. God created sex, and wise is the person who permits the Creator to make the rules.

Unnatural female discharges (vv. 25-33). A prolonged hemorrhage would be both physically painful and religiously disastrous, for the woman would be perpetually unclean. The unknown woman who came to Jesus for help had suffered with this affliction for twelve years (Mark 5:25-34; Luke 8:43-48). Strictly speaking, everybody she touched in that big crowd was defiled by her whether they knew it or not; when she touched our Lord's garment, He was also defiled. How gracious of Him to heal her and give back to her the normal life she longed for! The ritual for her cleansing reminds us of the ritual for the restoration of a mother after the birth of a baby (Lev. 12:6-7).

These regulations for personal sanctity weren't just pious suggestions from the religious leaders of the nation. They were holy commandments from the Lord, and it was a serious thing to disobey them (15:31-33). For an unclean person to go to the tabernacle would be to defile the tabernacle and invite judgment (v. 31). God warned the Israelites that a violation of the law given in Leviticus 15:24 would cause the couple to be "cut off from among their people" (20:18). Whether "cut off" meant death (it's used that way in Gen. 9:11) or excommunication, commentators don't agree, but whatever the penalty was, it was serious.

God's people today don't live under the threat of such judgments, although "there is a sin unto death" (1 John 5:16; see 1 Cor. 11:30). But there should be no area in our lives from which God is excluded, and every relationship should be under His control.

His words to us are still, "Be holy, for I am holy!"

Israel's High and Holy Day

The most important day of the year for the Old Testament Jew was the Day of Atonement — Yom Kippur — when God graciously atoned for all the sins of all the people and gave the nation a new beginning. Because today they have neither a temple nor a priest (Hosea 3:4), Israel can't celebrate Yom Kippur in the appointed way, but those who have received Jesus Christ can see in this ancient ritual a picture of what Jesus did for us on the cross.

1. An appointed time (Lev. 16:1-2, 29)

The deaths of Nadab and Abihu (Lev. 10) must have put the fear of God into Aaron and the priests so that they wondered whether it was even safe to enter the tabernacle's precincts to do their work. God made it clear that the priests needed not be afraid to serve, but that only the high priest was to enter the holy of holies, and that only once a year on the Day of Atonement. It wasn't a matter of human choice; it was a matter of divine appointment. Any priest who disobeyed would die.

The appointed day was the tenth day of the seventh month (16:29; 23:26-32; 25:9; Num. 29:7-11). The Jewish calendar is described in Leviticus 23, and we'll study it in detail in chapter 10, but we need to notice now the importance of the seventh month (our mid-September to mid-October). On the first day of the seventh month, the trumpets were blown to announce the beginning of a new year (Rosh Hashanah; 23:23-25).¹ The tenth day was the Day of Atonement (23:26-32), and then came the Feast of Tabernacles (or Booths), which started on the fifteenth day of the month and lasted a week (23:33-44).

The blowing of the trumpets announced the new year, but only the shedding of the blood could give the people forgiveness and a new beginning. "Without the shedding of blood there is no forgiveness" (Heb. 9:22, NIV). There was certainly sin in the camp. In addition, not every offender had brought the required sacrifices the previous year, and the sanctuary itself had been defiled in ways only God could see. It was time for a new beginning.

The high priest had to repeat the ritual of the Day of Atonement year after year, but Jesus Christ came at the right time (Gal. 4:4-5) to finish the work nobody else could do. "Once at the end of the ages, He has appeared to put away sin by the sacrifice of Himself" (Heb. 9:26, NKJV). The death of Christ on the cross has fulfilled the Day of Atonement.

2. An announced purpose (Lev. 16:30-34)

The Hebrew word *kapar*, translated "atonement," is used sixteen times in Leviticus 16; and it basically means "to ransom, to remove by paying a price." The priest placed his hands on the head of the sacrifice, symbolizing the transferring of the nation's sins to the innocent victim who died in their place. Atonement means that a price is paid and blood is shed, because life must be given for life (17:11). John Stott says it magnificently: "We strongly reject, therefore, every explanation of the death of Christ which does not have at its center the principle of 'satisfaction through substitution,' indeed divine self-satisfaction through divine self-substitution."[2]

The word "blood" is used nine times in this chapter and thirteen times in chapter 17. If the Day of Atonement teaches us anything about salvation, it's that there can be no salvation from sin apart from the shedding of blood. Those who reject this view and claim that they want "only the loving religion of Jesus" had better listen to what Jesus Himself said: "For this is My blood of the New Covenant, which is shed for many for the remission of sins" (Matt. 26:28, NKJV). "Just as the Son of Man did not come to be served, but to serve, and to give His life a ransom for many" (Matt. 20:28, NKJV).

The sacrifices offered on the Day of Atonement brought a threefold cleansing: to the high priest and his family (Lev. 16:6, 17), to the people of Israel (v. 17), and to the tabernacle (vv. 16, 20, 33). It seems strange to us that the holy sanctuary would be defiled and need cleansing, but such was the case. The sins of the people not only defiled themselves, but they also defiled the tabernacle of God. The sacrifices made on earth purified the earthly sanctuary, but our Lord's sacrifice purified "the heavenly things" with the blood of a better sacrifice (Heb. 9:23).

3. An afflicted people (Lev. 16:29, 31)

Regardless of the day of the week on which it fell, the annual Day of Atonement was considered a Sabbath, and the people weren't allowed to do any work. God commanded them to "afflict themselves" ("deny yourselves," NIV), a Hebrew word that means "to humble or oppress." It's used to describe the pain that the Egyptians inflicted on the Hebrews (Ex. 1:11-12) and the suffering Joseph felt in prison (Ps. 105:18). The "affliction" on the Day of Atonement is usually interpreted to mean fasting and the confession of sin.

On that day, God called His people to get serious about sin; the church needs to heed that call today. "Draw near to God and He will draw near to you. Cleanse your hands, you sinners; and purify your hearts, you double-minded. Lament and mourn and weep! Let your laughter be turned to mourning and your joy to gloom. Humble yourselves in the sight of the Lord, and He will lift you up" (James 4:8-10, NKJV).

"Repentance is almost a lost note in our preaching and experience," said Vance Havner, "and the lack of it is filling our churches with baptized sinners who have never felt the guilt of sin or the need of a Savior. . . . We are trying to get young people to say, 'Here am I' before they have ever said, 'Woe is me!'"

The fact that the people weren't to do any work reminds us that we are saved wholly by God's grace, through faith, and not because of our character or our good works (Eph. 2:8-9). The forgiveness that the people received that day was the gift of God.

4. An assigned procedure (Lev. 16:3-28)

It wasn't enough that the high priest serve on the right day, for the right purpose, and that the people have the right heart attitude. It was also important that the high priest follow the right procedure that God gave to him. The Day of Atonement was not a time for innovation because too much was at stake.

The high priest prepares (vv. 3-5). First of all, the high priest had to make sure the proper sacrifices were available: a bull and a ram for himself and his family, and two goats and a ram for the people. These animals had to be examined to make sure they had no defects.

The high priest then took off his glorious garments, washed at the laver, and put on the simple linen garments of an ordinary priest. He left his special garments in the holy place, where he would return later to put them on again.

Laying aside his glorious robes was an act of *humiliation,* and washing at the laver was an act of *sanctification.* He was setting himself apart to serve the Lord and His people on this special day.

In a much greater way, our Lord Jesus Christ did all of this for us. "And for their sakes I sanctify Myself, that they also might be sanctified through the truth" (John 17:19). He never needed to be cleansed from sin because He was sinless, but He did set Himself apart to serve us. He laid aside His glory and came into this world as a poor baby. As God's Suffering Servant, He humbled Himself and died on the cross (2 Cor. 8:9; Phil. 2:5-11). His work completed, He returned to heaven and "dressed Himself" once again in the glory that is rightfully His (John 17:1, 5).

The high priest offers his own sin offering (vv. 6, 11-14). Being now properly washed and dressed, the high priest then went to the altar where he sacrificed the bull as a sin offering for himself and his family, which probably included all the priests (Lev. 16:11). Taking some of the blood of the bull, plus a censer of coals from the altar and a supply of the special incense, he entered the holy of holies. He put the incense on the coals so that the cloud would cover the mercy seat upon the ark (v. 13), and then he sprinkled some of the blood *on* the mercy seat and some of the blood seven times *before* the mercy seat (v. 14).

Since the cloud of incense symbolized the glory of God, the high priest put God's glory ahead of everything else. It reminds us of Christ's first request in His high priestly prayer, "Glorify thy Son, that thy Son also may glorify Thee" (John 17:1). We need to remember that the ultimate goal of God's great plan of salvation is not the good of people but the glory of God (Eph. 1:6, 12, 14). The high priest needed a sacrifice because he was a sinner, but Jesus didn't need a sacrifice for Himself because He is sinless (Heb. 7:23-28).

The high priest offers the sin offering for the people (vv. 7-10, 15-22). The two goats together constituted *one* sin offering ("two kids of the goats for a sin offering," Lev. 16:5), even though only one goat was slain. The high priest cast lots over the goats, and one of them was chosen to die. He killed the goat and took some of its blood into the holy of holies, where he sprinkled it on the mercy seat and seven times before the mercy seat, just as he'd done with the blood of the bull. But he also sprinkled the goat's blood in the holy place of the tabernacle and applied it to the horns of the brazen altar, along with the blood of the bull. Thus he purified the tabernacle and altar "from the uncleanness of the children of Israel" (v. 19).

The high priest then put both hands on the head of the living goat and confessed "over it all the wickedness and rebellion of the Israelites—all their sins" (v. 21, NIV). This goat was led out of the camp and released in the wilderness, never to be seen again.

This goat is called "the scapegoat" (vv. 8, 10, 26), short for "escape-goat," that is, the goat that escaped death and escaped into the desert.[3] The Hebrew word is *azazel,* which could be a compound of the two Hebrew words "goat" and "to go away." Some Hebraists connect it with an Arabic word that means "to remove, to banish." Regardless of the origin of the word, the meaning is clear: The releasing of the goat symbolized the sins of the people being carried away, never to be held against them again. "As far as the east is from the west, so far has He removed our transgressions from us" (Ps. 103:12, NKJV). "Behold! The Lamb of God who takes away the sin of the world!" (John 1:29, NKJV)

Remember that the two goats were considered *one* sin offering (Lev. 16:5). One goat died because there must be blood sacrifice before there can be forgiveness. The other goat lived but was "lost" in the wilderness, having "carried away" the nation's sins. Because the living goat was part of a sin offering, the man who led the goat out of the camp had to wash himself and his garments before he could return to the camp (v. 26).

The high priest washes himself and puts on his official garments (vv. 23-24). Once he was sure that the scapegoat was officially lost in the wilderness, the high priest went into the holy place of the tabernacle, took off the linen garments, bathed, and put on his official robes. This reminds us of our Lord's return to heaven, where He received the glory He had laid aside when He was here on earth.

The high priest offers the burnt offerings (vv. 3, 5, 24). He offered a ram for himself and a ram for the people, each a symbol of total devotion to the Lord. At the same time, he burned the fat of the sin offering (see 4:8-10). "But there is forgiveness with You, that You may be feared" (Ps. 130:4, NKJV). Forgiveness and the fear of the Lord go together, for the privilege of forgiveness carries with it the obligation of commitment and obedience. Jesus offered Himself up to the Father in total obedience, and we cannot do less than follow His example.

Once the burnt offerings had been presented, and the fat of the sin offerings burned, the high priest supervised the carrying of the sin offerings outside the camp to be burned (Lev. 4:1-12; see Ex. 29:13-14). The man who did the job had to wash before he could return to the camp.

5. An appropriate picture (Zech. 12:10–13:1)

Many see in the annual Day of Atonement a picture of Israel's future cleansing when their Messiah appears to deliver them, cleanse them, and establish them in their kingdom.

The seventh month begins with the blowing of the trumpets, and there is a future "trumpet call" for Israel to gather the people together. "And it shall come to pass in that day that the Lord shall thresh, from the channel of the River to the Brook of Egypt; and you will be gathered one by one, O you children of Israel. So it shall be in that day. That the great trumpet will be blown; they will come, who are about to perish in the land of Assyria, and they who are outcasts in the land of Egypt, and shall worship the Lord in the holy mount at Jerusalem" (Isa. 27:12-13, NKJV). Jesus also refered to this future gathering of the Jews (Matt. 24:29-31).

Just as the Day of Atonement was a day of personal "afflicting" for the Jews, so they will mourn when they see their Messiah (Zech. 12:10-14). God will give them "the spirit of grace and supplication" (v. 10), and they will repent of their sins and believe in Him. "They will look on Me, the One they have pierced, and they will mourn for Him as one mourns for an only child" (v. 10, NIV).

Israel's repentance and faith will lead to their cleansing. "On that day a fountain will be opened to the house of David and the inhabitants of Jerusalem to cleanse them from sin and impurity" (13:1, NIV). Their Messiah who died for them will be their sin offering and burnt offering, and they will make a new beginning as a forgiven people, beloved of the Lord. What the Lord said about the Jewish remnant returning home from Babylon will be true of the nation in that great day: "Search will be made for Israel's guilt, but there will be none, and for the sins of Judah, but none will be found, for I will forgive the remnant I spare" (Jer. 50:20, NIV).

The annual Day of Atonement was followed by the Feast of Tabernacles, Israel's most joyful time of celebration, and Israel's future "Day of Atonement" will be followed by the establishing of the kingdom God promised to His people (Isa. 11–12; 32; 35). Creation will be delivered from the bondage of sin (Rom. 8:18-22); Jesus will reign as King, and "in His days the righteous will flourish; prosperity will abound till the moon is no more" (Ps. 72:7, NIV).

Holiness Is a Practical Thing

In his famous commencement address given at Harvard University on June 7, 1978, Russian novelist and social critic Alexander Solzhenitsyn said, "I have spent all my life under a Communist regime, and I will tell you that a society without any objective legal scale is a terrible one indeed. But a society with no other scale but the legal one is not quite worthy of man either."

With all due respect to hardworking legislators, judges, law-enforcement officers, and lawyers, I agree with Solzhenitsyn; it takes more than good laws to make good people and a good society. In our world today, not everything that's legal is moral or biblical. Some human activities that courts sanction and society defends, God will one day judge as abominable sin.

Leviticus 17–20 constituted a legal code for the people of Israel, touching on many areas of their personal and public life. The emphasis isn't simply on justice or civic righteousness, as important as they are, but on *holiness*. After all, Israel was *God's* people and the law was *God's* law. The Lord said to them, "Sanctify yourselves therefore, and be holy, for I am the Lord your God. And you shall keep My statutes, and perform them: I am the Lord who sanctifies you" (20:7-8, NKJV).

The motivation for Israel's obedience had to be more than fear of punishment. The people also needed *in their hearts* a desire to please God and a determination to be a holy people who would bring glory to His name (Ex. 19:3-6). Obeying the law and having holy character aren't necessarily the same thing.

Twenty-four times in these four chapters you find the declaration, "I am the Lord!" God was giving His people divine laws that expressed His holy will, laws that He expected them to respect and obey. While obedience to the law isn't God's way of salvation (Rom. 3:19-20; Gal. 3:21-29), a love for holiness and a desire to obey and please God are certainly evidences that we are the children of God (1 John 3:1ff).[1]

These chapters deal with four special areas of life that must be respected and kept holy: the sanctity of blood, or life (chap. 17); the sanctity of sex (chap. 18); the sanctity of the law (chap. 19); and the sanctity of judgment (chap. 20).

1. The sanctity of blood (Lev. 17:1-16)

According to Leon Morris, the word "blood" is used 460 times in the Bible, 362 of them in the Old Testament.[2] In Leviticus 17, you find the word "blood" 13 times; you also find in this chapter the key text in biblical theology on the significance of the blood in salvation: "For the life of the flesh is in the blood, and I have given it to you upon the altar to make atonement for your souls; for it is the blood that makes atonement for the soul" (v. 11, NKJV).

Long before medical science discovered the significance of the circulation of the blood in the human body and its importance for life, Scripture told us that the blood was the life. When a sacrifice was offered and its blood was shed, it meant the giving of a life for the life of another. The innocent victim died in the place of the guilty sinner. Throughout Scripture, it's the blood that makes the atonement. Any theology that ignores or minimizes the blood isn't founded on the Word of God.

The offering of food (vv. 1-7). The Jews didn't eat a great deal of meat because it was too costly to slaughter their animals. The law stated here prohibited them from killing their animals for food anywhere inside or outside the camp. Any animal used for food had to be brought to the altar and presented as a fellowship (peace) offering to the Lord.

This law accomplished several things. To begin with, it kept the people from secretly offering sacrifices to idols out in the fields. If they were discovered and questioned, they could claim that they were killing the animal only for a feast. But if that were the case, they should have taken the animal to the tabernacle altar. The blood of an animal must be offered only to the Lord and only at His altar.

Second, by this law the Lord dignified ordinary meals and made them a sacred experience. The slain animal wasn't just a piece of meat; it was a sacrifice presented to the Lord. According to verse 4, slaying an animal away from the altar was the same as murdering the animal, and God wants us to treat His creation with greater respect. When we thank God at the table for our food, we're not acknowledging only His goodness; we're also sanctifying the meal and making eating it a spiritual experience.

Third, by bringing the animal to the altar, the offerer was seeing to it that the Lord (3:1-17) and the priest (7:11-18) each received their rightful portion. To be sure, the offerer wouldn't get as much meat for himself and his family, but the principle behind Matthew 6:33 would compensate him in other ways. The fellowship meal at the house of God would glorify God and satisfy the needs of the offerer and those who ate with him.

The offering of sacrifices (vv. 8-9). This is a further application of the first law; even if you were bringing a legitimate sacrifice to God, it had to be brought to the altar and the blood shed there. No Jew was ever allowed to offer a sacrifice in the fields or at his tent. There was one tabernacle, one altar, and one ordained priesthood, and the people had to respect God's orders.

These laws were modified slightly when the nation went into the land of Canaan (Deut. 12:1-16). In the camp of Israel, nobody would be too far from the door of the tabernacle. Thus bringing an animal for a fellowship offering wouldn't pose a problem. But in the land of Canaan, distance would create a problem. Therefore, the Lord allowed the people to kill animals for food at home without having to bring them to the altar (vv. 15-16). However, all *sacrifices* had to be at the altar, and nobody was permitted to eat the blood.

The eating of blood (vv. 10-14). Because the blood is the life of the creature and the God-ordained means of atonement, it must not be treated like ordinary food. This prohibition goes all the way back to Noah (Gen. 9:1-4) and was repeated often in the law (Lev. 3:17; 7:26-27; Deut. 12:16, 23-25; 15:23). The early church included this regulation in its instructions to Gentile converts (Acts 15:23-29). In many heathen religions, it was a common practice to use blood for food, which explains why God warned even the non-Jews in the camp not to violate this law. How easy it would be for a Jew to follow the bad example of his heathen neighbor and thus incur the wrath of God!

Before preparing his meal, a Jew out hunting had to be careful to drain out the blood of the animal or bird he had caught. The blood then had to be covered with earth, giving it a decent burial, as it were. Orthodox Jews today are very careful to purchase kosher meat from which the blood has been drained in the prescribed manner.

The eating of animals found dead (vv. 15-16). Since meat was scarce and expensive, the chance finding of a dead animal in the field might appear to be a favorable event. But the carcass was obviously unclean because the blood hadn't been drained out, and it had been exposed to whatever vermin were available. No Jew would want to take a chance in becoming unclean by eating the meat. If he did, he had to stay out of the camp until evening, then bathe himself and his clothing to be made clean.

Believers today need to appreciate the importance of the "precious" blood of Christ (1 Peter 1:19). Among other things, through His blood, we are justified (Rom. 5:9), redeemed (Eph. 1:7), washed (Rev. 1:5), sanctified (Heb. 13:12), brought near (Eph. 2:13), and cleansed (1 John 1:7). The church was purchased by the blood of Christ and therefore is very precious to God (Acts 20:28).

2. The sanctity of sex (Lev. 18:1-30)

We live in a sex-saturated society. It smiles at monogamous marriages, encourages abortion as a means of birth control, promotes and endorses kinky sex as a means of entertainment, claims that moral absolutes don't exist, and really believes that people can violate moral standards and escape the consequences. Fulton J. Sheen was right when he said, "The Victorians pretended sex did not exist; the moderns pretend that nothing else exists."

Authority (vv. 1-5). There are several reasons why the Lord gives clear instructions concerning personal sexual hygiene, sexual morality, and marriage. For one thing, we're created in the image of God, and the Creator knows what's best for His creation. God certainly wants married couples to enjoy the beautiful gift of sex, but He also wants them to avoid the terrible consequences that come when His laws are violated.

God had chosen Israel to be the channel through which His

Son would come into the world, and it was important that the channel be sanctified. The breakdown of marriage in the Jewish society and the adopting of pagan practices could threaten the plan of God for their redemption. This seems to be the emphasis of Malachi 2:15. The Lord was "seeking godly offspring" (NIV) that can come only from godly marriages.

A Christian marriage should be a witness to the world of the love Christ has for His church (Eph. 5:25-33), but if that marriage isn't pure and faithful, the witness is destroyed. If husbands and wives can't love each other as Christ loves the church, why invite their unsaved friends to be saved and share in Christ's love?

Three times in this passage God said, "I am the Lord" (Lev. 18:2, 4-5). The phrase is used forty-two times in Leviticus 18–26. That's all the authority we need for the standards that we hold! The Lord warned Israel not to look *back* and imitate the sins they saw in Egypt, nor to look *around* and imitate the sins of the Gentile nations (18:3). When the Jews entered Canaan, they would discover that the people there were unspeakably immoral; Israel would have to maintain a position of separation in order to be pleasing to the Lord. The church today must maintain that same position (2 Cor. 6:14–7:1; Eph. 5:1-14; Col. 3:1-7).

Obedience to God's commandments brings life (Lev. 18:5). Indeed, other biblical writers often quoted this verse (see Neh. 9:29; Luke 10:28; Rom. 10:5; Gal. 3:12). If people could *perfectly* obey God's law, their obedience would save them, but, of course, nobody can. Therefore, salvation is wholly by faith, totally apart from the works of the law (Rom. 3:19-31). However, after we're saved, our obedience to the will of God, as revealed in the Word of God, is the basis for fellowshipping with God and enjoying the abundant life He wants us to have.

Standards (vv. 6-23). Since God invented sex and ordained marriage, He has every right to establish the regulations that control them, and our obedience will help protect these wonderful blessings from the defilements of the world. The *laissez faire* attitude of the humanistic world that says "anything goes" is not for the Christian. When it comes to moral standards, we're becoming more and more of a persecuted remnant, but we dare not retreat.

The repeated phrase "uncover the nakedness" simply means "to have sexual relations with." These laws would apply not only to marriage but also to casual contacts that were immoral. The prohibitions are listed in this chapter; the penalties are spelled out in chapter 20.

Leviticus 18:7-18 deal with incestuous relationships. These regulations are based on the fact that, in marriage, the man and woman are one flesh (Gen. 2:21-25; 1 Cor. 6:16; Eph. 5:31). A person who had relations with his stepmother, for example, would be "uncovering the nakedness" of his father; for the father and stepmother would be one (Lev. 18:8; see 1 Cor. 5:1ff). Most modern societies prohibit consanguineous marriages, not because of what the Bible says but because of the consequences of such unions. There is a tendency for their children to inherit the recessive detrimental genes and bring out the worst in the family tree rather than the best.

Leviticus 18:16 did not prohibit what is known as "levirate marriage." ("Levir" is the Latin word for "husband's brother.") This occurred when a deceased husband's brother married the widow so as to beget sons who would continue the family name and protect the family inheritance (see Deut. 25:5-10). The law stated in Leviticus 18:16 prohibited only illicit relations between brother-in-law and sister-in-law.

The seventh commandment, "You shall not commit adultery" (Ex. 20:14, NKJV), is expressly stated in Leviticus 18:20 (see Deut. 5:18). A man might argue, "I can enjoy my neighbor's wife because she isn't a relative, so it's legal." But God said it was wrong, and that settled it. The Bible repeats the stern warnings against adultery (see Prov. 2:16-19; 7:5-22; Matt. 5:28; Rom. 13:9; Gal. 5:19; James 2:11).

The warning about Molech (Lev. 18:21) will be dealt with when we study 20:1-5.

This section climaxes with prohibitions against homosexuality (18:22) and bestiality (v. 23; see Ex. 22:19; Deut. 27:21), with the warning that these sins are defiling, detestable (NIV), and a perversion (NIV). The best commentary is Romans 1:24-32 (see also Gen. 18:16–19:38; Jud. 19; Deut. 23:17-18, where a male cult prostitute is called a "dog").

That people who have committed any of these sins can be forgiven and become God's children is clear from Matthew 12:31 and 1 Corinthians 6:9-11; that God expects them to repent and forsake their old lifestyle is clear from 2 Corinthians 5:21, Ephesians 5:1-10, and Colossians 3:1-7.

Consequences (vv. 24-30). The picture here isn't a pretty one. Sexual perversions are like disease germs; they make a society and a nation sick. Then the land itself becomes sick and must vomit out its filthy people the way a human body vomits out poison. How tragic that people made in God's image should end up as vomit! Please note that these were *Gentile* nations that were judged—peoples with whom God had not made any covenants, but He still held them accountable for their filthy deeds against nature (Rom. 1:18ff).

If God so dealt with *Gentile* nations, to whom He'd never given His law, how much more will He hold accountable those who claim to know Him and possess His Word? There are dire consequences to sexual sins, and the judgment is greatest where the light has been the brightest. Alas, the nation of Israel disobeyed God, defiled their land, and were vomited out into captivity. Today, there are both secular and religious organizations that openly espouse an immoral lifestyle contrary to God's Word; in God's eyes, they're making society sick.

83

3. The sanctity of law (Lev. 19:1-37)

In chapter 19, the Ten Commandments are applied to various areas of life; in chapter 20, the penalties are stated that must be imposed on those who disobey His commandments. God expected His people to take His law seriously and to apply the penalties obediently and without favoritism.

The regulations given in chapter 19 aren't arranged in any discernible order, but the one thing that ties them together is their relationship to the Ten Commandments (Ex. 20:1-17), which is the basis for all Jewish law and should be the basis for all moral law. Perhaps the easiest way to classify these laws is to see them in their relationship to God, to others, and to things.[3]

Precepts relating to God. Since He is a holy God, we must be a holy people (Lev. 19:1-2). We've noted that the phrase "I am the Lord your God" is repeated over forty times in Leviticus 18–26 to remind us that we belong to Him. He warns us, "Fear your God: I am the Lord" (19:32, NKJV). Note that God calls these laws *"My* statutes" and *"My* ordinances" (v. 37), that the Sabbath is *"My* Sabbath" (vv. 3, 30) and the tabernacle is *"My* sanctuary" (v. 30). The law brings sinful people into the presence of a sovereign God who has every right to tell us what is right and wrong.

Honoring the Sabbath (vv. 3, 30) reminded them of the fourth commandment (Ex. 20:8-11) and of the fact that the Sabbath was a special "sign" between God and Israel (31:13-17; Neh. 9:13-14). When we study Leviticus 23, we'll discover that Jewish life was based on a system of sevens, beginning with the seventh day.[4] Violating the Sabbath Day was a capital offense (Num. 15:32-36).

The law against *idolatry* (v. 4) focuses on both the first and second commandments (Ex. 20:2-6), and it carried the death penalty (Lev. 20:1-5). We could include here the prohibition against indulging in *the occult* (vv. 26, 31), a form of idolatry that Scripture clearly condemns (Deut. 13:1-5; 18:9-22).

Leviticus 19:5-8 emphasizes the importance of *following God's instructions for worship*. He told them how to present the peace offering (3:1-17; 7:11-21), and He expected them to obey. We can also include 19:27-28, which are prohibitions against *imitating the practices of unbelievers*. Christians today may consider styles and fashions morally neutral, but this isn't always the case. While Christians shouldn't look like they came from "out of this world," they certainly ought not to imitate the world. "Be not conformed to this world" (Rom. 12:2, KJV).

The name of the Lord (v. 12) is sacred and must never be used blasphemously or in an oath that the person has no intention of fulfilling. This is the import of the third commandment (Ex. 20:7). If we fear the Lord, we'll respect His name and sincerely pray, "Hallowed be Thy name" (Matt. 6:9).

Precepts relating to others. These begin with *respect for one's parents* (Lev. 19:3), which is the fifth commandment (Ex. 20:12; Matt. 15:3-6; Eph. 6:1-4). Related to this is *respect for the aged* (Lev. 19:32), for God is concerned about the elderly (Isa. 46:4; 1 Tim. 5:1-2, 4, 8; 1 Peter 5:5), and we should be too. God is also concerned for those with *physical handicaps* (Lev. 19:14). Jesus healed the blind and the deaf; we can't do that, but we can help protect them and enable them to live better lives. God is also concerned for *strangers in our midst* (vv. 33-34), and He often reminded the Jews that they had been strangers in Egypt (Ex. 22:21; 23:9; Lev. 25:23; Deut. 10:19). When you consider the thousands of foreign students who attend our colleges and universities, a mission field at our doorstep, this admonition becomes even more significant.

God's concern for *the poor and needy* is seen in the "harvest laws" (Lev. 19:9-10; see 23:22; Deut. 23:24-25; 24:19-22; Ruth 2). It is also seen in the regulation about *wages* (Lev.

85

19:13). Since workers were paid daily, any delay would cause hardship (Deut. 24:14-15; James 5:4), and employers must never take advantage of their employees. *Rich and poor* stand equal before God and the law, and justice must not be partial (Lev. 19:15; see Ex. 23:3), because God hears the cries of the poor when they are oppressed (Ps. 82:3-4). The nation must be careful to have *just weights and measures,* lest unscrupulous merchants rob innocent people (Lev. 19:35-36; see Prov. 11:1; 16:11; 20:10, 23; Amos 8:5; Micah 6:10-11).

The eighth commandment says, "You shall not steal" (Ex. 20:15, NKJV); the ninth commandment warns against lying (v. 16), and both are included in Leviticus 19:11. Respect for *truth* and for *property* is the foundation for a just and orderly society. The *liar and talebearer* (v. 16) is a menace to public safety and peace, particularly if he or she is a lying witness in court.

Sexual morality is demanded in verses 20-22 and 29. The phrase "she shall be scourged" is translated "there must be due punishment" in the NIV, which could mean the offender had to pay the woman's fiancé an amount of money. It is difficult to understand why a Jewish father would want his daughter to become a prostitute in a pagan temple (v. 29; Deut. 23:17). Both of these laws apply to the seventh commandment, "You shall not commit adultery" (Ex. 20:14, NKJV).

Getting along with people, especially our neighbors, isn't a matter of obeying laws but of having love in our hearts (Lev. 19:18). "Love is the fulfilling of the law" (Rom. 13:10). The new commandment to love one another helps us handle human relationships and treat people the way God treats us (John 13:34-35).

Precepts relating to things. The strange regulation in Leviticus 19:19 seems to prohibit imitating practices related to heathen worship, or, it may simply be a reminder that Israel

is a separated people. Hebrew scholar R. Laird Harris translates the first clause, "Do not make your animals fall down
with an unequal yoke." This would parallel Deuteronomy
22:10. It would be cruel to yoke to the same heavy load two
animals of unequal stature and strength.

That God is concerned about ecology is seen in Leviticus
19:23-25, and note also Deuteronomy 20:19-20. Fruit, of
course, can't be "circumcised"; the word simply means "forbidden." By the fourth year, the fruit would be more mature,
since it would be the third crop since planting; this belonged
to God. The firstfruits should always be His (Prov. 3:9-10).

4. The sanctity of judgment (Lev. 20:1-27)
This chapter states the penalties imposed on those who
broke God's law. The same Lord who declared the precepts
also declared the penalties.

Fifteen offenses in Israel were capital crimes: striking or
cursing a parent (Ex. 21:15, 17); breaking the Sabbath
(31:14); blaspheming God (Lev. 24:10-16); engaging in occult
practices (Ex. 22:18); prophesying falsely (Deut. 13:1-5);
adultery (Lev. 20:10); rape (Deut. 22:25); unchastity before
marriage (vv. 13ff); incest (Lev. 20:11-12); homosexuality (v.
13); bestiality (vv. 15-16); kidnapping (Ex. 21:16); idolatry
(Lev. 20:1-5); false witness in a case involving a capital crime
(Deut. 19:16-21); killing a human intentionally (Ex. 21:12).

The people of Israel were the covenant people of God.
Therefore, the Law of God was the law of the land. Except
perhaps in some Muslim societies, there isn't a crime in the
above list that would merit capital punishment in most nations today, including murder. But the biblical view of law is
different from the modern view. God gave His law to restrain
sin, not to reform sinners; the penalties He imposed were for
the purpose of upholding His law, not improving the offenders. However, this doesn't mean that Christians today should

lobby for the death penalty for all these offenses. While we want to do what we can to see just laws enforced justly, our main task is winning people to Christ and our main weapons are the Word of God and prayer (Acts 6:4).

The Jews usually stoned capital offenders to death (Lev. 20:2; Deut. 13:10; 17:5; 22:21, 24), but Leviticus 20:14 and 21:9 speak of offenders being burned with fire. We're not sure what the phrase "cut off" means (20:3, 5-6, 17-18); in some places, it seems to be equivalent to being killed. It may also have meant expulsion from the camp and the loss of all covenant privileges. Some offenders God inflicted with childlessness (vv. 20-21), and of others He said, "They shall bear their iniquity" (v. 19).

Molech (vv. 1-5) was the god of the Ammonites. His metal image was heated red hot and little children were placed in his arms and burned to death (see 2 Kings 23:10; 2 Chron. 33:6; Jer. 32:35). People who practiced such idolatry were inhuman, and their presence in the camp defiled God's sanctuary and profaned His holy name. Idolaters were not tolerated because they influenced others and led people away from the worship of the true God.

The offenses mentioned in this chapter have been dealt with in our study of Leviticus 18–19, particularly those relating to sexual sin. Note that this chapter closes with another reminder that the sins of the people can defile the land (20:22-27). This warning looked forward to the time when Israel would enter Canaan and claim her inheritance. As a chosen and separated people, they were obligated to make a difference between the clean and the unclean and not to live like the pagans around them.

While law can be a light that exposes evil and a guard that restrains evil, it can never change the human heart. Only the Gospel of Jesus Christ can do that. God has ordained authorities to keep peace and order in society (Rom. 13); Christians should obey the law, do good, and pray for those in office. God's moral law is the revelation of His holy will for humanity, and individuals and nations can't despise God's law and escape judgment.

Over two centuries ago, the American patriot Thomas Jefferson wrote in his *Notes on the State of Virginia,* "Indeed, I tremble for my country when I reflect that God is just."

Sober words for us to reflect on today.

The Cost of Spiritual Leadership

Whether it's manufacturing cars, waging wars, selling computers, or building the church, everything depends on leadership. God's people are "all one in Christ Jesus" (Gal. 3:28) and equal before God, but we're different in our gifts, abilities, and our special callings.

The spiritual leaders in the nation of Israel were the priests. "He shall not defile himself, being a chief man among his people" (Lev. 21:4, NKJV). They were in charge of the sanctuary of God; they taught the people the Word of God; they offered the sacrifices on God's altar; when called upon, they determined the will of God for the people. Apart from the ministry of the priests, Israel had no way to approach God.

The priests had to meet the qualifications God gave for the priesthood, and they had to serve Him according to His directions. In their personal conduct, physical characteristics, and professional concerns, they had to meet God's approval. There's a price to pay if you want to be a spiritual leader.

1. Personal conduct (Lev. 21:1-15)

The privilege of leadership brings with it the responsibility of maintaining a life that's above reproach. In their devotion and obedience to God, the priests were to be examples to the rest of the nation.[1] Unfortunately, the priesthood in Israel declined spiritually and led the people astray. "They feed on the sins of My people and relish their wickedness. And it will be: Like people, like priests. I will punish both of them for their ways and repay them for their deeds" (Hosea 4:8-9, NIV).

There were qualifications and requirements not only for the priests but also for every member of the priests' families. The important thing for all of them was that they remain ceremonially clean before the Lord. The word *defile* is used four times in this chapter, and the word *profane* is used eight times. You will notice that at the end of each major paragraph in chapters 21–22, the Lord says, "I am the Lord who sanctifies you," or words to that effect (Lev. 21:8, 15, 23; 22:9, 16, 32).

The high priests's sons (vv. 1-8). There was only one high priest, but since his sons served with him, they were also ordained and required to meet the qualifications given by the Lord. Other Jews in the camp could plan weddings and funerals pretty much as they pleased, but God told the priests how to express their grief (vv. 1-6) and how to select a wife (vv. 7-8).

During Bible times, expressing grief was an art form practiced by people who were specialists in mourning (Gen. 50:7-11; 2 Chron. 35:25; Mark 5:38). While God expected the priests to show sorrow at the death of a loved one, He also expected them to act like the servants of God.[2] Anyone who touched a dead body, or even went into a tent where somebody had died, was defiled for a week, and defilement would prevent the priest from serving the people (Num. 19:11-14). Therefore, the priests could defile themselves only for their parents, their children, and their brothers and unmarried sisters, but all other deceased were off-limits for them. Obedience had to take precedence over affection.

But the Lord even regulated the *manner* of their grief (Lev. 21:4-6; see 19:27-28). These forbidden practices were the customs of the pagan peoples around Israel, and God's people aren't supposed to "sorrow . . . as others which have no hope" (1 Thes. 4:13). Even in our grief, we must seek to glorify God.

Any priest who shaved his head and his beard and who cut his body (1 Kings 18:28) was acting like the heathen and thereby profaning God's name and defiling God's altar. A priest who acted like his pagan neighbors would encourage the Jewish people to disobey God's law and follow his bad example. It was indeed a privilege for him to know God and serve at God's altar. To disobey God would mean dishonoring God's name and defiling God's altar and sacrifices.

Whenever I'm asked to participate in the ordination of a pastor or the commissioning of a missionary, I've tried to encourage the candidate to focus on the privileges of ministry and not on the burdens and sacrifices. Jesus Christ is not a hard taskmaster and "His commands are not burdensome" (1 John 5:3, NIV). No priest should have complained because of these restrictions. After all, he was serving the Lord and the Lord's people, a privilege well worth any sacrifices he might have to make.

As for marriage, the priests were forbidden to marry prostitutes and divorcees. In the pagan religions, there were temple prostitutes serving with the priests, but prostitution was forbidden in Israel (Lev. 21:9; see 19:29; Deut. 23:17). Since a priest's sons would hold a special place in the nation, he would have to be careful not to marry a woman who might bring alien progeny into the family. The only way to be sure the priestly line was kept pure was for him to marry a virgin.

When you read the qualifications for pastors (elders, bishops) and deacons in 1 Timothy 3 and Titus 1, you can't help but see that a church officer's wife and family are an important part of his ministry. During more than forty years of ministry, I've met more than one Christian worker who's had to "go it alone" in his service because his wife had no interest in spiritual things. All believers must be careful in choosing mates (1 Cor. 7:39; 2 Cor. 6:14-18), but those who have been called to serve Christ must be even more vigilant.

The priest's daughter (v. 9). If his daughter became a prostitute and lived a wicked life, the priest didn't lose his ministry, but the daughter lost her life. She was probably stoned to death (Deut. 22:21) and then her corpse humiliated by being burned like common trash (Josh. 7:25; see Lev. 20:14). In the church today, the elder must be one whose "children believe and are not open to the charge of being wild and disobedient" (Titus 1:6, NIV). This requirement may appear to be unnecessarily severe, but "if anyone does not know how to manage his own family, how can he take care of God's church?" (1 Tim. 3:5, NIV)

The high priest (vv. 10-15). Since the high priest was especially anointed and clothed with holy garments (8:7-12; 16:4), he had a greater obligation to serve the Lord faithfully and honor His name. The ordinary priests were permitted to be defiled by the dead bodies of their immediate family, but the high priest wasn't allowed to do even that. Nor was he allowed to manifest grief in the usual ways or to leave the tabernacle precincts for a burial (see 10:6-7). Aaron and his sons had their tents on the east side of the tabernacle (Num. 3:38), and they were expected to stay on duty and not become involved in other activities in the camp (see 2 Tim. 2:4).

Since the firstborn son of the high priest became the next high priest, it was important that no alien issue invade the family; hence, the high priest could marry only a virgin (Lev. 21:13-14). In most cases, the priests chose their wives from the tribe of Levi (Luke 1:5), and this would be especially so with the high priest. To marry an unfit woman would defile his offspring, and this would defile the priesthood which the Lord God had sanctified (Lev. 21:8, 15).

While these special regulations don't apply to workers in the church today, the principles are still important and applicable. If we want to have God's blessing on our ministry, we must keep ourselves, our marriages, and our families pure and dedicated before God. A godly marriage with godly children constitutes a spiritual fortress from which God's servants can go forth to do battle for the Lord. Christians need to pray much for pastors and other spiritual leaders, and their families, because those who lead are special targets of the enemy.

2. Physical characteristics (Lev. 21:16-24)

Everyone born into Adam's race is a sinner, suffering from the tragic consequences of Adam's fall, but our physical and moral defects aren't an obstacle to either salvation or service. When God invites the lost to be saved, He calls to "the poor, the crippled, the blind and the lame" (Luke 14:21, NIV), the very people Jesus ministered to when He was here on earth (Matt. 4:23-25). And all believers can surrender to the Lord and be "living sacrifices" for His glory, no matter what handicaps they may have.

Fanny Crosby, the great hymn writer, was blind; so was George Matheson, author, hymn writer, and preacher. Amy Carmichael directed the work of her mission in India from her sickbed. The Scottish Presbyterian preacher Robert Murray McCheyne was often prostrated by his weak heart. And Charles Spurgeon had to leave London in the winter to restore his health in the south of France. Physical handicaps need not be a barrier to Christian service if we depend wholly on the grace of God (2 Cor. 12).

In the nation of Israel, however, God required that every

priest be free from defects and blemishes. There were two reasons for this requirement. First of all, the sacrifices that the people brought to the Lord had to be perfect; it was only right that those who offered the sacrifices at the altar also be without defect. Second, the priests exemplified that great High Priest who was to come, and there is no defect in Him.

We have no reason to believe any disqualified priest was treated like a second-class citizen in the camp of Israel. While priests with physical defects couldn't serve at the altar or in the holy place, they were still considered priests and were allowed to share with their families in the sacrificial meals (Lev. 2:3, 10; 6:14-18) and the other material benefits that the tribe of Levi enjoyed.

We're not sure of the meanings of all the Hebrew words for the defects named in this paragraph, but "blind or lame, disfigured or deformed" seems to summarize them (21:18, NIV). Some of these would be birth defects; others might be the sad consequences of sickness or accidents. The ancients weren't as skillful in setting broken bones or dealing with diseases as physicians are today. The "broken stones" in verse 20 refers to damaged testicles. Eunuchs weren't permitted in the worshiping community of Israel (Deut. 23:1) and certainly wouldn't be allowed to minister at the altar. The begetting of children was important to the Jews, and it was especially important that the priestly line be perpetuated.

Once again, this biblical passage must not be used today to humiliate or intimidate anybody with a physical disability. It was never written for that purpose. The priests were special people with an important job to do, and God wanted them to be the very best physically. A beautiful soul often lives in a crippled body, and people like that can be greatly used of the Lord.

The next time you hear a recording of the great conductor Arturo Toscanini, remember that he owed his success to a handicap: He was nearsighted. At the age of nineteen, while playing the cello in a small European orchestra, he had to memorize the complete score because he was seated in the orchestra pit where he couldn't see the music well enough to read it. One day the leader became sick, and Toscanini was the only one available who knew all the music. Thus he conducted the concert completely from memory. This was the beginning of his remarkable career, all made possible by a handicap — and a good memory.

3. Professional concerns (Lev. 22:1-33)

For a priest to serve the Lord acceptably, it wasn't enough merely that he qualify as a son of Aaron without any physical defects. He also had to carry on his ministry in such a way that the Lord was pleased with him. The worshipers might look at the outward ritual, but God would look at his inner heart.

The phrase "separate themselves from the holy things" (v. 2) sets the theme for the chapter. It means "to treat with regard and respect" or "to be careful in handling." The priests offered sacrifices all day long, all year long; it would be easy for them to develop an attitude of "professionalism" that would turn a sacred ritual into a shallow routine. Novelist George MacDonald said, "Nothing is so deadening to the divine as an habitual dealing with the outsides of holy things." That's what this warning is all about.

When I was a seminary student, one of my professors told us of his concern when he heard the conversation between two students calling to each other across the campus one afternoon.

"Where are you going?" the first one asked.

"Over to Madison Avenue!" came the reply.

"What's going on there?"

"Oh, I have to read over a stiff!"

96

The professor was both angry and hurt to think that one of his students would describe a Christian funeral service as "reading over a stiff." This attitude is what Ralph G. Turnbull called "the specter of professionalism," being able to go through the motions of ministry but your heart isn't in it.[3] Outwardly, you do all the right things the right way, but when God looks at your heart, nothing there is right. By the time of Malachi the prophet, the specter of professionalism overshadowed the work of all the priests (Mal. 1:6–2:9).

Carelessness and professionalism at the altar would show itself in three ways: unclean priests (Lev. 22:3-9), unqualified guests (vv. 10-16), and unacceptable sacrifices (vv. 17-33). The priest would end up defiling himself, the sacrifices, and the very altar where he was supposed to serve God.

Unclean priests (vv. 3-9). Suppose a priest became defiled but did nothing about it? How would anybody know that he was unclean? He could minister at the altar, handle the sacrifices, even eat his lawful share of the sacred offerings, and apparently get away with it. But God would know it, and the priest would be in danger of death (v. 9).

This kind of behavior would indicate that the priest was putting himself ahead of God and was more concerned about his reputation than his character. The name for this sin is *hypocrisy.* It worried him that the people would know he was unclean, but it didn't worry him that he was defiling the sacred ministry for which God had set him apart. Like the Pharisees in our Lord's day, this priest appeared to be clean but was actually "toxic" (Matt. 23:25-28).

All who serve the Lord and the Lord's people must be open and honest before God and must minister first of all to please Him alone. We must thank God for the privilege of being called to serve, and we must treat the things of God with holy respect. "Nothing in all creation is hidden from God's sight. Everything is uncovered and laid bare before the eyes of Him to whom we must give account" (Heb. 4:13, NIV). Joseph took that approach when he said to his temptress, "How then can I do this great wickedness, and sin against God?" (Gen. 39:9) This was also Paul's approach to ministry: "So I strive always to keep my conscience clear before God and man" (Acts 24:16, NIV).

The greatest protection against professionalism and hypocrisy in ministry is the fear of the Lord as revealed in a tender conscience (2 Cor. 1:12; 4:2; 5:11). Conscience is like a window that let's in the light. When the window becomes soiled, the light gradually becomes darkness. Once conscience is defiled (Titus 1:15), it gradually gets worse, and eventually it may be so "seared" that it has no sensitivity at all (1 Tim. 4:2). Then it becomes an "evil conscience" (Heb. 10:22), one that functions just the opposite of a good conscience (1 Peter 3:16).

Unqualified guests (vv. 10-16). A priest could eat portions of specified offerings and share the food with those in his family who were qualified to eat, but if he was too generous with God's offerings and included outsiders, he sinned against the Lord and against his guest. The unqualified guest would have to bring a trespass offering plus a fine, and this would make that meal a very expensive one indeed!

In other words, a faithful priest had to have the honesty and courage to say no both to himself (Lev. 22:1-9) and to others (vv. 10-16). This would include any daughters who had married outside the priestly family (vv. 12-13). His loving heart would want to include them in the feast, but he wasn't allowed to do so. To include them would only hurt them and force them to pay a fine.

One of the most difficult things in Christian ministry is having to say no, but to keep our fellowship pure before God, we must sometimes do it. The pastor who refuses to marry a believer to an unbeliever often makes enemies, especially among their relatives, but he keeps his conscience pure before God. Parents who forbid their children to cultivate damaging friendships are misunderstood and sometimes maligned, but they know they're doing the will of God. Churches that refuse to receive into membership people who give no evidence of saving faith in Christ are often called "holier than thou," but they have the courage to say no.

Unacceptable sacrifices (vv. 17-32). Just as the priests had to be free from physical defects, so the sacrifices that they offered had to be perfect or the Lord wouldn't accept them. I wonder how many times the priests had to reject a worshiper and his sacrifice because the man was trying to give the Lord an inferior animal that wasn't worth keeping and couldn't be sold? " 'When you bring injured, crippled or diseased animals and offer them as sacrifices, should I accept them from your hands?' says the Lord" (Mal. 1:13, NIV). " 'Try offering them to your governor! Would he be pleased with you? Would he accept you?' says the Lord Almighty" (Mal. 1:8, NIV).

Not only must God's servants not make it easy for people to sin (Lev. 22:10-16), but also they must encourage people to give their best to the Lord. David's attitude was right: "I will not sacrifice to the Lord my God burnt offerings that cost me nothing" (2 Sam. 24:24, NIV). The priest who had respect for his ministry and high regard for the sacrifices of God would accept only those animals that met God's requirements. To send a worshiper away from the altar with a false assurance of forgiveness would be to do great damage to his or her spiritual life.

The special requirement about the age of the offering (Lev. 22:26-28; see Ex. 22:30) shows the tender heart of the Creator toward His creation (Jonah 4:11; Deut. 22:6-7). A calf or lamb younger than a week old who was transported any distance to the sanctuary might die in the process. It seems to me that it would be cruel to kill the mother and her young on the same day, for whatever purposes. In fulfilling our religious duties, we must be careful not to be heartless and uncaring in the way we use what God provides for us. More than one social critic has pointed out that the way people treat animals gradually becomes the way they treat humans. "For whatever happens to the beasts, soon happens to man," said Native American Chief Seattle. "All things are connected."

Suppose a priest asked, "Why should I honor and respect the sacrifices of God and the ministry He has given me?"

The closing three verses of this chapter would clearly answer that question.

(1) These are God's commandments, and they must be obeyed. God never commands anything that isn't the best for us.

(2) This is the way we glorify God's great name and sanctify Him before His people.

(3) The Lord who commands us also redeemed us from slavery, and He's the one who has set us apart to be His special people. We owe everything to Him!

What greater motivation do we need?

N I N E

The Calendar that Tells the Future

If you want to enter a world of disorder and bewilderment, study the development of the modern calendar.

By the time of Julius Caesar, the calendar was so out of step with nature that Caesar ordered a Greek astronomer named Sosigenes to straighten things out. Unable to alter the movements of the heavens, Sosigenes solved the problem by temporarily adding nearly three extra months to the calendar, giving the year 46 B.C. 445 days! The people born that year must have had fun later on trying to figure out their birthdays.

Pope Gregory XIII (1502–85) commissioned the calendar we use today. In fact, it is a revision of the old Julian calendar. When Great Britain and its colonies adopted the Gregorian calendar in 1752, September 3 became September 14, and eleven days disappeared from British history. Twenty-year-old George Washington found his birthdate moved from February 11 to February 22. Perhaps he celebrated his birthday twice a year.

Calendars are a normal part of our modern busy world, but they weren't that important to the people of Israel in Moses' day. The Jews worked from sunrise to sunset, counted the months by the phases of the moon, and watched the seasons come and go. God had promised them "seedtime and harvest, and cold and heat, and summer and winter, and day and night" (Gen. 8:22), and they were content. Each day was a sacred gift from God.

God gave Israel a calendar that was tied to the rhythm of the seasons and the history of the nation. It was an unusual calendar because it not only summarized what God had done for them in the past, but it also anticipated what God would do for them in the future. The salvation work of Jesus Christ, the founding of the church, and the future of the people of Israel are all illustrated in these seven feasts.

In this chapter, these special days are called "feasts" nine times and "holy convocations" ten times. "Feasts" have nothing to do with eating. In fact, on the Day of Atonement, the people fasted. The word simply means "appointed times." "Convocation" gives the idea that during each of these feasts, all the people met together as a congregation, but this also was not true. There were special gatherings on some of the special days, but the word basically means "proclamation" or "announcement." The Lord "appointed and announced" these events, which the people faithfully had to celebrate.

1. The weekly Sabbath: God orders our times (Lev. 23:1-3)
The weekly Sabbath wasn't one of the annual feasts (Ex. 20:8-11), but it was an important day for the Jewish people, and they were expected to honor it. To dishonor it meant death (Num. 15:32-36).

God gave the Sabbath to Israel for several reasons. For one thing, it provided needed rest and refreshment for the people, the farm animals, and the land. ("Sabbath" comes from a Hebrew word that means "to rest, to cease from labor.") Based on Genesis 2:1-3, the weekly Sabbath reminded the Jews that Jehovah God was the Creator and they were but stewards of His generous gifts. The Lord also ordained Sabbath years and the Year of Jubilee to keep the Jews from exploiting the land and impoverishing it (Lev. 25). God's tender concern for His creation is seen in the Sabbath laws.

The Sabbath was also a special sign between God and His covenant people (Ex. 31:12-17). Other peoples might work on the seventh day and treat it like any other day, but the Israelites rested on the seventh day and thereby gave witness that they belonged to the Lord (Neh. 13:15-22; Isa. 58:13-14). Nehemiah made it clear that the Sabbath law wasn't given to Israel until they arrived at Sinai (Neh. 9:13-14), while Psalm 147:19-20 indicates that the law was never given to the Gentile nations. Although believers today aren't commanded to "remember the Sabbath Day" (Rom. 14:1ff; Col. 2:16-17), the principle of resting one day in seven is a good one.

2. Passover: Christ died for our sins (Lev. 23:4-5)

Passover is Israel's feast of deliverance; the key passage is Exodus 12. The innocent lamb died for the firstborn; because the blood of the lamb was applied to the door by faith, the firstborn sons were safe. This was "the Lord's passover" and the only means of deliverance that He provided that awesome night when the death angel visited Egypt. To reject the blood of the lamb was to accept judgment and death.

The lamb typified Jesus Christ, who shed His blood on the cross for a world of lost sinners (John 1:29; 1 Peter 1:19-20). "For even Christ our passover is sacrificed for us" (1 Cor. 5:7). Since the Passover lamb had to be perfect, it was chosen on the tenth day of the month and watched carefully until it was slain on the fourteenth day of the month. Jesus Christ "knew no sin" (2 Cor. 5:21), "did no sin" (1 Peter 2:22), and "in Him is no sin" (1 John 3:5).

The firstborn Jews in Egypt weren't saved from death by admiring the lamb, caring for the lamb, or loving the lamb.

The lamb had to be slain, and the blood applied to the door-posts of each Jewish house. We aren't saved by Christ the Example or Christ the Teacher. We're saved by Christ the Substitute, who gave His life in our stead on the cross at the same hour the Passover lambs were being slain at the Jewish temple in Jerusalem.

The Jews also fed on the lamb, and this gave them strength for the journey ahead of them. No outsider was permitted to eat the Passover feast (Ex. 12:43-51). You had to be either born into the family (vv. 48-49) or purchased, and the men had to bear on their body the mark of the covenant. Those who have never trusted Jesus Christ can't "feast" on Him through the Word and find the strength they need for the journey of life. Only somebody born into God's family through faith in Christ, purchased by His blood and marked by the Holy Spirit as a child of the New Covenant, can appropriate Jesus Christ through the Word and "feed" on Him.

Passover was the beginning of the Jewish religious year (vv. 1-2); and when sinners trust Christ, it marks for them a new beginning in a new life (2 Cor. 5:21). Israel was not only delivered from judgment; the nation was also delivered from Egypt and set free to go to their promised inheritance.

3. Unleavened Bread: separation from sin (Lev. 23:6-8)
For seven days following Passover, the Jews ate only unleavened bread with their meals, and they carefully cleansed all the yeast out of their homes (Ex. 12:15-20). In many places in Scripture, leaven depicts sin. Thus the putting away of leaven illustrates the cleansing of one's life after he or she has been saved through faith in the blood (2 Cor. 6:14–7:1).

We must get rid of the "old life" leaven (1 Cor. 5:7). Those things belong to our unconverted days and have no place in our new Christian walk (1 Peter 4:1-5). We must also put away "the leaven of malice and wickedness" (1 Cor. 5:8; Eph.

4:31-32), the leaven of hypocrisy (Luke 12:1), and the leaven of false doctrine (Gal. 5:7-9). The "leaven of Herod" (Mark 8:15) represents the attitude of pride and worldliness that was evident in that evil king's life. And the "leaven . . . of the Sadducees" was unbelief (Matt. 16:6).

The people weren't saved from death and bondage by getting rid of leaven but by applying the blood of the lamb by faith. People today think they'll be saved because they reform or get rid of a bad habit, but good as doing these things are, they can never do what only the blood of Christ can do. Salvation is through the blood of Christ alone, the sinless Lamb of God, but "let everyone who names the name of Christ depart from iniquity" (2 Tim. 2:19, NKJV).

The Christian life is not a famine or a funeral; it's a feast. "Therefore let us keep the feast . . . with the unleavened bread of sincerity and truth" (1 Cor. 5:8). Sin can be secretly introduced into our lives and quietly grow so that it pollutes the inner person. One "toxic" Christian in a church body can defile the whole body if given enough time. One false doctrine, if allowed to grow, will destroy an entire ministry.

In many parts of the Western world, you will find churches and schools that once were true to the Christian faith but today deny that faith. How did this happen? At some point a board hired a professor or called a pastor who didn't wholeheartedly agree with the evangelical statement of faith, and the yeast of false doctrine was quietly introduced. Before long, the whole lump of dough was leavened, and the ministry was no longer evangelical. Christian leaders must be on their guard and courageously seek to keep God's work as free from leaven as possible.

4. Firstfruits: Christ raised from the dead (Lev. 23:9-14)

The day after the Sabbath that followed Passover, which would be the first day of the week, the priest took the first sheaf of barley from the field and waved it as an offering before the Lord. It was a token that the first and the best belonged to God, and it was done before Israel reaped the harvest for themselves (Ex. 23:19; Neh. 10:34-37; Prov. 3:9). It was also an expression of gratitude to the Lord for giving the harvest and supplying their daily bread. The Jews weren't allowed to eat of the harvest until the firstfruits had been given to the Lord (Lev. 23:14), an Old Testament picture of Matthew 6:33.

The male lamb sacrificed as a burnt offering spoke of the nation's dedication to God. The meal offering and drink offering were reminders that their two dietary staples, bread and wine, came from God (see Ps. 104:14-15).

There is a deeper meaning to this ceremony, however, for Jesus Christ is "the firstfruits of them that slept" (1 Cor. 15:20). Jesus compared His death and burial to the planting of a seed (John 12:23), and Paul carried the image further by seeing His resurrection as the harvest of the grain (1 Cor. 15:35-49).

Two basic truths emerge here. First, God accepted the sheaf for the whole harvest, and because the Father accepted Jesus Christ, we are accepted in Him (Eph. 1:6). Second, the sheaf is like the harvest. The priest didn't wave palm branches to represent the barley harvest; he waved a sheaf of barley. As the firstfruits of the resurrection harvest, Jesus Christ is now what one day His people shall be. At the "resurrection harvest," we shall be like Him (1 Cor. 15:49; Phil. 3:20-21; 1 John 3:1-3).

The fact that this ritual took place on the first day of the week, the Lord's Day, is significant, for Jesus Christ arose from the dead on the first day of the week. Psalm 118:17-24 seems to describe the resurrection victory of Messiah over all His enemies (see Matt. 21:1-11, 42-46), and Psalm 118:24 says, "This is the day which the Lord hath made; we will rejoice and be glad in it." This could be a reference to the first day of the week, resurrection day.

5. Pentecost: birthday of the church (Lev. 23:15-21)

This special day was also called "the Feast of Weeks," because it was celebrated seven weeks after firstfruits. The word "Pentecost" means "fiftieth," and since the feast was held seven weeks after firstfruits, it too was on the first day of the week, the Lord's Day. Each Lord's Day commemorates the resurrection of Christ, the coming of the Spirit, and the birth of the church.

Instead of the priest waving *sheaves* before the Lord, he waved two *loaves* of bread baked with leaven. In order to have loaves, the grain had to be ground into flour and the flour baked into loaves. The fulfillment of this image is recorded in Acts 2 when fifty days after Christ's resurrection, the Holy Spirit came and united the believers into the church, symbolized here by the two loaves (Jews and Gentiles).[1] There's leaven in the two loaves because there's sin in the church (Lev. 2:11). The church will not be "holy and without blemish" (Eph. 5:27) until it sees the Lord in glory.

The feast lasted only one day, a day on which the people were not to work but were to rejoice before the Lord and bring Him an offering commensurate with the harvest He had given them (Deut. 16:9-12). This event would have marked the end of the wheat harvest, and the Jews were commanded to remember the poor as they harvested the grain God had generously given them (Lev. 23:22; see Deut. 24:19-22). Because of this commandment, Ruth was able to glean in the field of Boaz (Ruth 2). As a result, she married Boaz, and eventually David was born (Ruth 4).

Along with the wave loaves, thirteen different animal sacrifices were presented to the Lord: seven lambs, a young bull, and two rams for a burnt offering (dedication); a kid of the goats for a sin offering (atonement); and two lambs for a peace offering (reconciliation, fellowship). Unless Jesus Christ had died, been raised from the dead, and then returned to heaven, the Holy Spirit could not have come to earth to minister. All of these sacrifices were fulfilled in His one offering on the cross (Heb. 10:1-18).

God's people can't function properly in this world apart from the ministry of the Holy Spirit. It is the Spirit who baptizes believers into the body of Christ (Acts 1:5; 1 Cor. 12:13) and empowers them for service and witness (Acts 1:8; 4:8, 31), enabling them to endure persecution and suffering for the glory of God.

Following the Feast of Pentecost, there's a four-month gap on God's calendar before the next feast. This gap could represent the age we're now in, the age of the church, during which we should be devotedly involved in the harvest (Matt. 9:36-38) and eagerly waiting for the sound of the trumpet (1 Cor. 15:51-58; 1 Thes. 4:13-18).

6. Trumpets: the calling of God's people (Lev. 23:23-25)
The final three feasts were celebrated in the seventh month, our modern September–October. The number seven is important in this calendar and in God's plan for Israel (Dan. 9:20-27). There are seven feasts, three of them in the seventh month. The Sabbath is the seventh day of the week. Pentecost is fifty days after firstfruits (seven times seven plus one). The Feast of Unleavened Bread and the Feast of Tabernacles each lasted seven days.

The Hebrew word for "seven" comes from a root word that means "to be full, to be satisfied." It's also related to the word meaning "to swear, to make an oath." Whenever the Lord "sevens" something, He's reminding His people that what He says and does is complete and dependable. Nothing can be added to it.

According to Numbers 10:1-10, the priests blew the silver trumpets for three occasions: to call the people together, to announce war, and to announce special times, such as the new moon. The Feast of Trumpets was held on the first day of the seventh month and ushered in the new civil year (Rosh Hashanah, "the head of the year"). The sacrifices for the Feast of Trumpets are listed in Numbers 29:1-6.

The Scottish preacher Alexander Whyte once said that "the victorious Christian life is a series of new beginnings." God gives His people opportunities for new beginnings, and we're foolish if we waste them. Unlike our modern New Year's Day celebrations, the Jews used the first day of their new year for prayer, meditation, and confession. They sought to make a new beginning with the Lord.

There's also a prophetic message to this feast. Because of their unbelief and rejection of Christ, Israel became a scattered people (Lev. 26:27-33; Deut. 28:58-67), but God will gather them again to their land in the last days (Isa. 11:1-12; 27:12-13; Matt. 24:29-31). When Israel was born into the community of nations on May 14, 1948, it reminded the world of God's ancient promises, and among the orthodox, "Next year Jerusalem!" became more than a Passover motto.

The basic interpretation of this feast relates to Israel, but we can make an application to the church. Some of the saints are in heaven and some are on earth, and those on earth are scattered in many tribes and nations. But all of us should be waiting expectantly for the sound of the trumpet and our "gathering together unto Him" (2 Thes. 2:1).

7. The Day of Atonement: forgiveness (Lev. 23:20-32)
We covered this important event in our study of Leviticus 16 in chapter 6. Note here the emphasis on the people afflicting their souls (fasting, praying, confessing sin) and abstaining from all work. "Not by works of righteousness which we

have done, but according to His mercy He saved us" (Titus 3:5).

As we noted in chapter 6, there's also a prophetic message to the Day of Atonement. After Israel is gathered to her land, the Jews will see their rejected Messiah, repent of their sins (Zech. 12:10–13:1), and be cleansed. The scattered nation will be gathered and the sinful nation will be cleansed. What a glorious day that will be!

8. Tabernacles: the joy of the Lord (Lev. 23:33-44)

The nation of Israel is not only a scattered people and a sinful people,[2] but they're also a suffering people. No nation in history has suffered as the Jews have suffered, but one day their suffering will be turned into glory and joy.

The Feast of Tabernacles (Booths) reminded Israel of God's blessings in the past (vv. 42-43). He had led them out of Egyptian bondage, cared for them in the wilderness, and brought them into their promised inheritance. Once they had lived in booths and tents, but in Canaan they would live in houses!

This feast was also called "the Feast of Ingathering" because it corresponded to the completion of the harvest (v. 39). Like Thanksgiving Day in the United States, it was a time of feasting, rejoicing, and giving thanks to God for His bountiful gifts (Deut. 16:13-15). But we must remember that *joy always follows cleansing* and that the Day of Atonement preceded this feast (see Ps. 51:12). People who want happiness without holiness are destined to be disappointed.

During the week of celebration, the priests followed an elaborate schedule of offering sacrifices (Num. 29), and by the eighth day, they had offered 199 animals! This was certainly a reminder that there can be no blessing apart from the grace of God and the sacrifice of His Son for us on the cross.

The Feast of Tabernacles pictures the future kingdom God

has prepared for Israel when their Messiah returns and they receive Him (Zech. 12:10–13:1; see Isa. 35; Luke 1:67-80). The Prophet Zechariah described the changes that will take place in the topography of the holy land and how the Gentile nations will celebrate the Feast of Tabernacles along with the Jews (Zech. 14:16-19).

For Israel, the best is yet to come! The scattered people will be gathered; the sinful people will be cleansed; the sorrowing people will rejoice. And for Christian believers, the best is yet to come; for we shall be together with the Lord and His people, every stain washed away, rejoicing in His presence.

It's worth noting that the Jews added two extra rituals to their celebration of the Feast of Tabernacles to remind them of God's wilderness blessings. The first was the pouring out of the water from the pool of Siloam, recalling God's provision of water in the desert; the second was the placing of four large lighted candlesticks to recall the pillar of fire that led the people by night.

Jesus related both of these traditions to Himself. It was during the Feast of Tabernacles, when the water was being poured out, that He cried out, "If any man thirst, let him come unto Me, and drink" (John 7:37). He also said to the temple crowd, "I am the light of the world" (John 8:12). What a tragedy the Jews were careful to maintain their traditions and yet completely missed their Messiah who was in their midst!

Each year, the grown males of the nation had to appear before God to celebrate three specific feasts: Passover and Unleavened Bread, Firstfruits, and Tabernacles (Ex. 23:14-19). These three feasts remind us of the death of Christ, the resurrection of Christ, and the return of Christ to establish His kingdom. Christ died for our sins; Christ lives; Christ is coming again! Hallelujah, what a Savior!

Holy, Holy, Holy

The most important structure in the camp of Israel was the tabernacle, the sanctuary where God dwelt and where the priests and Levites served Him. The outer covering of badgers' skins was not impressive, but within the tent of meeting, it was beautiful, costly, and glorious. It was the tabernacle that made the camp holy and set it apart for God, just as the presence of the Holy Spirit within believers sets them apart from the world and makes them wholly God's (1 Cor. 6:19-20; 2 Cor. 6:14-18; Eph. 1:13-14).

In this chapter, the Lord gave Moses instructions concerning three holy things: the holy oil for the lampstand (Lev. 24:1-4), the holy bread for the table (vv. 5-9), and the holy name of the Lord, which all the people were to honor (vv. 10-23).

1. The holy oil (Lev. 24:1-4)

The veil divided the tabernacle proper into two parts, the holy place and the holy of holies. In the holy place were three pieces of furniture: the golden altar of incense, the table of presence bread, and the golden lampstand. As the priest faced the incense altar, the table would be to his right and the lampstand to his left.

Since there were no windows in the tabernacle, it was necessary to have light in the holy place so the priests could see as they ministered there. The golden lampstand provided that light. It was hammered out of pure gold and made into one piece with a central shaft and six branches; pure olive oil fueled the lamps on the branches (see Ex. 25:31-39; 27:20-21; 30:7-8; 37:17-24; 40:24-25).

Each morning and evening, when the high priest burned incense on the golden altar, he was to care for the lights on the lampstand to make sure they would continue to burn.[1] Special golden instruments were provided for pulling up the wicks from the oil and trimming them.

The commandment in Leviticus 24:1-4 emphasized two essentials: (1) the people of Israel had to provide the olive oil regularly, and (2) it had to be beaten and pure (Ex. 27:20-21). There was a method of extracting olive oil by heat, but beating or crushing the olives and straining out the impurities produced the best olive oil. And the God of Israel deserves the very best.

Bible students generally agree that oil for *anointing* is a symbol of the Holy Spirit of God who anoints God's people for service (2 Cor. 1:21; 1 John 2:27), but this particular oil is for *burning* and not anointing. Zechariah 4:1-6 connects oil for burning with the Holy Spirit and identifies that lampstand as the two faithful servants of God. What does the tabernacle lampstand signify?

I personally think that the golden lampstand first of all symbolizes the Word of God, the light that God gives us in this dark world (Ps. 119:105, 130; 2 Peter 1:19). The unconverted can't see or understand the light of the Word of God because they lack the ministry of the Holy Spirit (1 Cor. 2:9-16). Nobody outside the holy place could see the light from the golden lampstand, but those within appreciated its light.

Apart from the light of the Word, God's servants can't see

where they are or what they're doing, nor can they serve God effectively. The lampstand gave light so the priest could burn the incense on the golden altar, and apart from the Scriptures, we can't pray effectively (Ps. 141:1-2; John 15:5; Acts 6:4). The light from the lampstand illuminated the beautiful hangings in the holy place and also revealed the bread on the golden table. The illuminating ministry of the Spirit of God makes the things of God real and clear to us.

I'd like to suggest that the lampstand could also symbolize the nation of Israel, as did the twelve loaves of bread on the golden table, which we'll study next. God called Israel to be a shining light in a very dark world, but they had to shine first of all in His presence before they could witness to their pagan neighbors (see Isa. 58:8; 60:1-3). The tragedy is that the priesthood became wicked and failed to maintain the nation's light before the Lord (1 Sam. 3).

Of course, Jesus is the light (Luke 2:32; John 1:4, 9; 8:12; 9:5), and only through Him can we see and appreciate spiritual things. The Apostle John compared local churches to individual golden candlesticks that are supposed to shine and bear witness in their cities (Rev. 1:12, 20; see Matt. 5:16; Eph. 5:8; Phil. 2:15).

If the people of Israel didn't bring the beaten olive oil, the lights couldn't be kept burning in the holy place. The people might say, "Well, we can't see the lampstand anyway, so what difference does it make?" The lamp wasn't there for the people to see but for God to see and for the priest to use as he carried on his ministry. *What happened in the presence of God was far more important than what happened elsewhere in the camp!* Sad to say, many a local church has had its light go out before both God and the world because of the unfaithfulness of the members. They failed to pray, give, and allow the Holy Spirit to use them. If the light is to be kept burning, somebody has to provide the oil.

2. The holy bread (Lev. 24:5-9)

Not only were the people to bring the pure olive oil for the lamp, but also they were to bring the fine flour out of which twelve loaves of bread were baked each week. These were put on the golden table each Sabbath, and then the old bread was given to the priests to eat.

The size of these loaves is a mystery to us because the text doesn't state the measure used in the recipe. The Hebrew simply reads "of two-tenths it shall be," but two-tenths of what? The NIV says "using two-tenths of an ephah," which would be about four quarts of flour, but the word "ephah" isn't in the Hebrew text. That much flour would produce a very large loaf, and it's doubtful that twelve large loaves would all fit on the table. It's probable that the loaves were stacked on top of one another, making two stacks of six loaves, with a small container of frankincense on top of each stack.

These loaves were treated like a "meal offering," complete with the frankincense (2:1-11). On the Sabbath, when the loaves were replaced, the priest would take a "memorial portion" from a loaf, add the frankincense, and burn it on the altar along with the daily burnt offering. The priests could then eat the old loaves, but they had to do it in the holy place (24:9).

What did this symbolize? Only the priests (the tribe of Levi) were allowed in the holy place, but the other tribes were *represented* there in two ways: by the jewels on the high priest's garments (Ex. 28:6-21), and by the twelve loaves on the table. The table was called "the table of shewbread" (Num. 4:7), and the loaves were called "shewbread" (Ex. 25:30), which can be translated "bread of presence." God was present with His people and they were in His presence in the tabernacle. No matter where the Jews were in the camp, they needed to remind themselves that their tribe was represented in the holy place on the golden table. The New Testament application would be Colossians 3:1ff.

From the priest's viewpoint, the loaves reminded him that his ministry was for real people. Being somewhat isolated in the tabernacle precincts day after day, the priests could easily get "out of touch" with the people they were representing before God. Oil from the people fed the lamp that gave the priests light, and the bread they ate each Sabbath came from flour given by the people. The twelve loaves reminded the priests that all the tribes were represented before God and were God's people. All of this should have made the priests more appreciative of the tribes and more anxious to serve them in the best way.

If there were only one loaf, it might be viewed as a type of Jesus Christ, the Bread of Life (John 6:35), but the imagery in John 6 is that of manna and not the loaves in the tabernacle. Matthew 6:11 also comes to mind: "Give us this day our daily bread." Whether we need spiritual bread for the inner person or physical bread for the body, we must look to God alone.

We expect to find oil and incense in the holy place, but not bread. After all, bread is a common food. But the presence of bread in the tabernacle assures us that God is concerned about the practical things of our lives and that there's no such thing as "secular" and "sacred" in the Christian life. It was this "presence bread" that David and his men ate when David was fleeing from Saul (1 Sam. 21:1-6; see Matt. 12:1-4).

3. The holy name of God (Lev. 24:10-23)

It may seem strange to us that the Book of Leviticus is interrupted at this point to tell about a blasphemer who was judged, but the narrative is an illustration, not an interruption. The basis for obedience to the law is the fear of the Lord, and people who blaspheme His holy name have no fear of God in their hearts.

Dishonoring God's name (vv. 10-11). Every Jew knew the third commandment: "You shall not take the name of the Lord your God in vain, for the Lord will not hold him guiltless who takes His name in vain" (Ex. 20:7, NKJV). So fearful were the Jews of breaking this commandment that they substituted the name "Adonai" for "Jehovah" when they read the Scriptures, thus never speaking God's name at all. To respect a name is to respect the person who bears that name, and our highest respect belongs to the Lord.

The blasphemer was the product of a mixed marriage between an Egyptian father and a Jewish mother from the tribe of Dan. Since the father isn't named as being present, we wonder if he had stayed in Egypt when the mother took her son and fled, or perhaps he was dead. This much is sure: The boy didn't grow up learning a proper respect for the Lord or His name. Even in Moses' day, marriages between believers and unbelievers created problems for God's people.[2] Moses had to contend with the bad influence of a "mixed multitude" who left Egypt at the Exodus but who really didn't have a heart for the things of the Lord (Ex. 12:38; Num. 11:4; see Neh. 13:23-31).

This Egyptian Jew got into a fight with a Jew in the camp (see Ex. 2:11-15), and during the fight he blasphemed the name of God. He may have cursed his adversary in the name of Jehovah or in his anger simply cursed the name of the Lord. Whatever is in our hearts will eventually come out of our lips (Matt. 12:34-35).

Of course, it's possible to blaspheme God's name in other ways beside swearing. Perjury dishonors God's name (Lev. 19:12), and so does stealing (Prov. 30:8-9). Jesus taught that our lives should be so pure that we won't need to use oaths or vows in order to make people believe us (Matt. 5:33-37). A multitude of words could be evidence that sin is present somewhere (Prov. 10:19).

Determining God's will (vv. 12-16). If a Jew had committed the awful sin of blasphemy, Moses would have known what to do, but this man was part Jewish and part Egyptian, and the law had nothing to say about this. Taking the wise approach, Moses put the man in custody and waited for the Lord to tell him what to do.

This is the first of four recorded occasions when Moses had to seek the mind of the Lord about special problems. The second occasion had to do with some men who had been defiled by a corpse and couldn't celebrate Passover. The Lord permitted them to celebrate the next month (Num. 9:6-14). The third occasion involved a man who had violated the Sabbath (15:32-36), and he was stoned to death. The fourth concerned the inheritance of the five daughters of Zelophehad whose question made it possible for Jewish women to inherit their father's land (27:1-11; 36:1ff). Note that in this last instance, one decision led to another, which is often the case when you are seeking the will of God.

Moses was humble enough to admit that he didn't know everything and had to ask the Lord what to do. That's a good example for leaders to follow in the church today. "The humble He guides in justice, and the humble He teaches His way" (Ps. 25:9, NKJV). God had given Israel all the laws they needed to govern their religious and civil life successfully, but Moses and the tribal leaders had to interpret these laws and apply them as new situations arose. When the leaders had no clear precept or precedent to follow, they had to seek the Lord's direction before they could give a correct opinion.

Immature Christians want the Lord to give them rules and regulations to cover every area of life, and this explains why they're immature. If we never have to pray, search the Scriptures, counsel with other believers, and wait on the Lord, we never will use our "spiritual muscles" and grow up. The Bible gives us precepts, principles, promises, and personal examples that together are adequate to guide us in the decisions of life. The motor club will give its members detailed maps for their trips, but the Bible is more of a compass that keeps us going in the right direction without spelling out every detail of the trip. "For we walk by faith, not by sight" (2 Cor. 5:7).

God instructed Moses what to do. The offender must be brought outside the camp where the entire assembly would stone him, for blasphemy was a capital crime in Israel (Matt. 26:65; Acts 6:11, 13; 7:58). Those who actually heard the man blaspheme would put their hands on his head to publicly identify him as the offender. The witnesses would also be the first to stone him (Deut. 17:7). In other words, the same law that applied to the Israelites also applied to the resident aliens (the "strangers" or "sojourners") who lived among the Jews (Lev. 24:16, 22). Even the "strangers" were not to blaspheme the name of the God of Israel.

Discerning God's mind (vv. 17-22). The Lord further applied this legal decision to other areas of life and laid down the principle that *the punishment must fit the crime* (see Ex. 21:22-25; Deut. 19:21). This is known as the *lex talionis,* "the law of retaliation," a principle that made sure the guilty offender was not punished more severely than the crime demanded. The murderer was to be put to death (Lev. 24:17, 21; Gen. 9:5-6), but the penalties for other crimes had to suit the offense.

Because this principle has been misunderstood, many people have called it cruel and unjust. They have questioned how a God of love and mercy could enunciate it. But this law was actually an expression of God's justice and compassion, because it helped restrain personal revenge in a society that had no police force or elaborate judicial system. Apart from this law, the strong could have crushed the weak at the least offense.

119

The Pharisees used the *lex talionis* to defend their practice of private revenge, a practice that Jesus condemned in the Sermon on the Mount (Matt. 5:38-39). Just as the *lex talionis* was a step forward from private revenge, so Matthew 5:38-39 is a giant leap forward from the *lex talionis*. However, we must keep in mind that our Lord's instructions in the Sermon on the Mount were given for believers, not unbelievers, and for individuals, not nations. In our modern courts, the principle of "make the penalty fit the crime" is still practiced.[3]

Dispensing God's justice (v. 23). Moses and the people went outside the camp and did as the Lord commanded. Today, many sincere people, both believers and unbelievers, would have opposed killing the offender, but the sentence was carried out. It was a capital offense, and the guilty man forfeited his life.

The arguments surrounding capital punishment are many and varied, but we must not make our personal opinions or convictions a test of fellowship or spirituality. The Law of Moses made a distinction between murder and manslaughter (Ex. 21:12-14) and provided six "cities of refuge," where an innocent man could be protected and get a fair trial (Num. 35). This arrangement frustrated the plans of angry relatives of the dead person, people who might want to take the law into their own hands.

In the Bible, murder is considered a serious crime. Humans are made in the image of God (Gen. 1:26-27; 1 Cor. 11:7; James 3:9), and to kill a human being is to attack God's image (Gen. 9:4-6). Life is a sacred gift from God, and only God can take it away or authorize it to be taken away. God has ordained human government and given civil authorities the power of the sword (Rom. 13:1-5). The purpose of capital punishment is not to frighten potential criminals into being good but to uphold and defend the law. It's a declaration that men and women are special — created in the image of God —

and that life is sacred in God's sight.[4]

Whether or not capital punishment affects the crime statistics isn't the main issue. It's doubtful that *any* of our laws are really deterrents to crime. Careless drivers still speed, people still park their cars in "no parking" zones, wage earners still cheat on their income tax, and burglars still steal. *But would any of us want our legislatures to repeal the laws against speeding, parking illegally, falsifying one's income tax, or stealing?* Of course not! Respect for truth, life, and property are cornerstones of a just and peaceful society. Capital punishment may not decrease the number of murders any more than speeding tickets decrease the number of speeders, but it does declare that humans are made in the image of God and that life is a sacred gift.

The Bible doesn't present capital punishment as a "cure-all" for crime. It presents it as a form of punishment that shows respect for law, for life, and for humans made in the image of God. To take a pragmatic or sentimental approach to the subject is to miss the point completely.

Leviticus 24 begins in the holy place of the tabernacle and ends outside the camp. It opens with oil and bread and closes with the shedding of guilty blood. But the emphasis is the same: Our God is a holy God and we must honor Him, whether in bringing our gifts or respecting His name. The Lord doesn't execute blasphemers today, but there is coming a day of judgment when the secrets of all hearts will be revealed, and then God will "render to every man according to his deeds" (Rom. 2:6).

"For there is no respect of persons with God" (v. 11).

"For whosoever shall call upon the name of the Lord shall be saved" (10:13).

This Land Is God's Land

The focus in chapters 25 and 26 is on *Israel in their land.* In fact, the word "land" is used thirty-nine times in these two chapters. The Lord's statement in verse 2 ("When you enter the land I am going to give you," NIV) must have been a great encouragement to Moses, especially after Israel failed to claim their inheritance at Kadesh-Barnea and had to wander in the wilderness (Num. 13–14).

If the Israelites were to possess and enjoy their land, they had to recognize and respect some basic facts, the first of which was that *God owned the land* (Lev. 25:2, 23, 38) and had every right to dispose of it as He saw fit. *God also owned the people of Israel* (v. 55), because He had redeemed them from Egyptian bondage. Because they belonged to Him, all the Jews were to treat one another as brothers and sisters (vv. 25, 35-38) and not take advantage of one another when it came to personal debts or property claims. The Jews were expected to toil in their fields, but it was *God who gave the increase* (v. 21) and supplied them with sunshine, rain, and harvests. In other words, the people of Israel had God as their "land Lord" and had to live by faith in His Word. This meant obeying His commandments and trusting His promises.

Another important fact emerges from this chapter: *God was in control of the calendar.* God not only gave His people their land and their food, but He also gave them special "times" to observe so that the land would not be ravaged and spoiled. God is concerned about ecology and the way we treat His creation. Like the ancient Jews, we today are but stewards of God's gifts; we must be careful not to abuse or waste them.

Had Israel obeyed these principles, their economic system would have functioned smoothly, the land would have provided all they needed, and everybody would have been cared for adequately. However, they didn't obey the Lord. The result was that the rich got richer, the poor got poorer, and the land was ruined.

1. Rest for the land: Sabbath Year (Lev. 25:1-7, 18-22)
When we studied Leviticus 23, we noted that the Jewish calendar was based on a series of sevens. There were seven annual feasts, three of them in the seventh month, and the seventh day of the week was the Sabbath, a day of rest. Now we learn that the seventh year was to be a year of rest for the land, the people, and their animals.

During the Sabbath Year, the people were not to work the fields or have organized harvests, but were to take from the fields the food they needed as it grew of itself. The people, including the poor and the aliens, could gather from the fields and be God's "guests" (Ex. 23:10-12).

Not only did the land rest, but also the people and the farm animals rested. The men certainly took care of the routine tasks that keep buildings from falling down, but they were not to engage in the normal activities of an agricultural society, like plowing, sowing, and harvesting. This prohibition also included the servants and the animals, all of whom were given a year of rest from their normal duties.

Deuteronomy 15:1-11 informs us that personal debts were

also remitted during the Sabbath Year and that indentured servants were set free. The word "release" in Deuteronomy 15:1 means "to let loose, to drop." It involves the canceling of debts and the freeing of slaves. As the people shared with the poor and with their liberated servants, they were to be generous and openhanded. Three motives were to govern what the people did: appreciation for God's blessings (Lev. 25:4, 6, 10, 14), appreciation for God's deliverance of the nation from Egypt (Deut. 15:15), and simple obedience to the command of God (v. 5). What God commanded was for the good of all the people, and nobody had the right to disobey Him. During the siege of Jerusalem by Nebuchadnezzar, King Zedekiah proclaimed a release for the slaves, but he later rescinded it (Jer. 34:8ff).

The Sabbath Year was also the occasion for a "Bible conference" when the priests read and explained the Book of Deuteronomy to all the people (Deut. 31:9-13). This was done during the Annual Feast of Tabernacles, which would usher in the new year. It would take a great deal of faith for the people to trust God for their daily food, and "faith comes by hearing, and hearing by the word of God" (Rom. 10:17, NKJV). During that special year, the nation learned the meaning of "give us this day our daily bread." God promised to protect them and provide for them throughout the year, if only they would trust and obey (Lev. 25:18-22).

We have no biblical evidence that the Jews ever celebrated the Sabbath Year, in fact, the Bible indicates that they didn't: "To fulfil the word of the Lord by the mouth of Jeremiah, until the land had enjoyed her sabbaths: for as long as she lay desolate she kept sabbath, to fulfil threescore and ten years" (2 Chron. 36:21). God sent Israel into Babylonian exile for seventy years in order to give the land the rest it needed (Jer. 25:8-11; 29:10). This suggests that for nearly 500 years, the Jews had disobeyed God's law concerning the Sabbath Year.

It's a basic principle of life that whatever we rob from God, we can never keep and enjoy ourselves. In my pastoral ministry, I've met people who robbed God of tithes and offerings, only to end up paying extra money for medical bills or car repairs. I recall one church member bringing his family budget book to my office, just to show me how God had begun to bless him when he stopped robbing the Lord. His figures showed that *every dollar he took from God had to be spent on some emergency need, and he never got to use that money himself.*

By disobeying the law of the Sabbath Year, the Jews robbed themselves not only of spiritual blessings but also of the strength of the land and of their servants and farm animals. By working the same land, year after year, they got their harvests, but they lost the renewal that comes from allowing the land to lie fallow and the workers to rest. They also lost the blessings that come from sharing with the needy, and they robbed God of the glory He would have received as the other nations saw how much He blessed His people. It was a costly mistake on their part, and they paid for it dearly.

2. Release and restoration: the Year of Jubilee (Lev. 25:8-17, 23-24)

The word "jubilee" is used five times in verses 8-17 and literally means "to sound the trumpet." (The Heb. word is *yobel,* which means "a ram's horn.") For the people of Israel, each new year opened with the blowing of the trumpets on the first day of the seventh month,[1] and ten days later, the people celebrated the Day of Atonement by fasting, repenting, and offering the required sacrifices. But every fiftieth year, at the close of the celebration of the Day of Atonement, the horns were blown again to announce that the Year of Jubilee had begun.

125

It would require a great deal of faith for the people to celebrate this special year, because the previous year—the forty-ninth—would have been a Sabbath year *when the fields, vineyards, and orchards would not have been cultivated.* The Jews had to trust God to provide for them for the forty-ninth and fiftieth years, and also during the fifty-first year while they waited for the harvest. God certainly wouldn't fail them, but their faith might fail. In fact, there's no evidence in Scripture that the nation of Israel ever celebrated the Year of Jubilee.

What elements were involved in the Year of Jubilee?

Repentance (v. 9). It's significant that the Year of Jubilee started with the Day of Atonement, a day when the Jews were commanded to "afflict themselves" and repent of their sins (16:29-34). They were not to enter the Year of Jubilee without the Lord first cleansing and forgiving them. If their hearts weren't right with God, they could never release their slaves or return the land to its original owners. Our relationship with God determines how we treat other people.

Release (vv. 10, 13). "Proclaim liberty throughout all the land unto all the inhabitants thereof" is inscribed on the Liberty Bell, which hangs in Independence Hall in Philadelphia. At the start of the Year of Jubilee, the people were commanded to release their indentured servants so that they might return to their own lands and families. A Hebrew servant was to serve for only six years and then be set free (Ex. 21:2). How could the Jews celebrate this special year if some of their people were in bondage and separated from their loved ones and their land?

Rest (vv. 11-12). During the Year of Jubilee, the people were forbidden to carry on their normal agricultural pursuits but had to live on whatever the land produced. This gave both them and the land an extra year of rest, since the previous year would have been a Sabbath Year. They had to rely on the Lord to keep His promises and supply sufficient food for almost three years, since they wouldn't be able to work the land until the fifty-first year; and even then, they'd have to wait for the harvest.

Restoration (vv. 13-17). Any property that was sold since the last Year of Jubilee would revert to its original owner, for the Lord wanted His land to remain with the tribes, clans, and families to which it had been allotted. For parents to care for their families, they had to have land to cultivate, and the private ownership of property gave stability to the economy. The Lord owned the land and only loaned it to His people. He wanted them to have a sense of proprietorship and responsibility in caring for His property. People usually take care of what they themselves own.

Whenever a piece of land was sold, the proximity of the next Year of Jubilee determined the price, for this determined how much produce the new owner could get from the soil. Since the buyer knew full well that the land would eventually revert back to the original owner, he certainly wasn't going to pay more for the land than what he would be able to get out of it. "The land shall not be sold forever" was God's law (Lev. 25:23).

These laws made it impossible for ruthless wealthy real estate speculators to accumulate vast land holdings and thus upset the economy. Even the poorest Israelite family received its land back, and by working the land, they could gain enough wealth to meet their needs and perhaps the needs of others. The Year of Jubilee provided a new beginning for the released slaves and the landowners, and this kept poverty and inequality to a minimum. The people were not to oppress one another (v. 17), but remember that the land was God's and they were only His tenants (vv. 23-24).

The Prophet Isaiah saw in the Year of Jubilee a picture of the promised messianic kingdom when the Lord would release His people and restore them to their land and bless them abundantly (Isa. 61:1-3). Jesus used this Isaiah passage as the text for the sermon He preached in the synagogue in Nazareth (Luke 4:16-30), and He applied it to the "acceptable year of the Lord" that He was inaugurating by His death and resurrection. Jesus stopped His reading at "the acceptable year of the Lord" ("the year of the Lord's favor," NIV) and didn't read the part about "the day of vengeance of our God." In Isaiah 6:2, this present "acceptable year" of God's grace is separated from the future "day of judgment" by a comma! God's wonderful "day of salvation" (2 Cor. 6:2) has lasted as long as it has because God is long-suffering and wants sinners to come to repentance (2 Peter 3:9, 15).

Like the announcement of the Year of Jubilee, the Gospel is good news to the poor, because their debts have been paid and are completely forgiven (Luke 7:36-50). All they need do is receive the Savior and rejoice in a new beginning. Just as the debtors and slaves were set free to enjoy Jubilee, so sinners are set free when they trust the Lord to save them. Salvation through faith in Jesus Christ is a "Jubilee" experience, for it restores broken families and lost blessings and brings "times of refreshing" from the Lord (Acts 3:19-21).

3. Redemption: the kinsman-redeemer (Lev. 25:25-55)
If a poor Jew had to sell himself or his property in order to stay alive, he didn't have to wait until the Year of Jubilee to regain either his property or his freedom. At any time, a kinsman who was willing and able to pay the price could redeem him or his land.

The redemption of land (vv. 25-28). If the former owner of the land was too poor to redeem his land, then a near kinsman could do it for him. But if the former owner somehow acquired the necessary wealth, he could redeem it for himself. The price would depend, of course, on the number of years (harvests) until the Year of Jubilee. If the man had neither a willing kinsman nor the necessary wealth, he would have to wait until the Year of Jubilee to regain his property.

The redemption of houses (vv. 29-34). A house in a walled city would be much more valuable than one in the open land because it afforded protection from invaders. The former owner had only one year in which to redeem the house. After that, it belonged to the new owner and wouldn't even revert to the original owner in the Year of Jubilee. After all, nobody would want to purchase an expensive house, move his family in, and then wonder how long he'd be living there!

Houses in unwalled villages could be redeemed at any time and would revert to the original owner at the Year of Jubilee. If a Levite sold his house in one of the forty-eight levitical cities (Num. 35; Josh. 21), he could redeem it at any time. If he didn't redeem it, the house would revert to him or his family at the Year of Jubilee. The Levites were given no tribal land allotment because the Lord was their inheritance (Josh. 13:14, 33; 14:3-4; 18:7), but they were given pasture lands adjacent to their cities (Num. 35:1-5). These lands could not be sold. (However, see Acts 4:34-37.)

The redemption of the poor (vv. 35-55). Moses deals with three possible scenarios.

A bankrupt brother in debt (vv. 35-38) could expect his "brother" Jews to assist him with an interest-free loan;[2] for the Jews were to treat one another compassionately, like members of the same family. The Jews were allowed to charge interest to Gentiles (Deut. 23:19-20). Since any debt incurred would be remitted during the Year of Jubilee, assisting others was truly an act of faith. However, the Lord had been so good to Israel in redeeming the nation from Egypt, allowing them to spoil the Egyptians and giving Israel the land of Canaan, that no Jew should want to exploit his fellow Jew. "Freely ye have received, freely give" (Matt. 10:8). The early church was quick to pick up this principle and put it into practice in helping widows and other needy believers (Acts 2:44-47; 4:34–5:1; 6:1-7; see Deut. 10:18; 24:17).

A poor brother who became the slave of a Jew (vv. 39-46) could be expected to be treated like a hired worker and not a slave. His master was to treat him and his family with kindness; for the Jews were once slaves in Egypt, and the Lord graciously delivered them. How could a Jew enslave a brother whom the Lord had set free? A Jewish slave was to serve only six years and go free at the Sabbath Year (Ex. 21:2); but if the Year of Jubilee came first, he was a free man.

The Jews were allowed to own slaves from the Gentile nations around them or the aliens living in their land (Lev. 25:44-46), but a Jew could never enslave a fellow Jew. Slaves were considered the property of the owner and could be made a part of the family inheritance. In other words, Gentile slaves had no hope of being set free, unless they could secure the purchase price, or the master decided to set them free.

During the Civil War era, some Americans used passages like these to prove that it was biblical and right for people to own and sell slaves. But it must be noted that God's laws didn't *establish* slavery; they *regulated* it and actually made it more humane. Slavery was an institution that had existed for centuries before Moses gave the law, and the Law of Moses forbade the Jews to enslave one another. God had to eliminate slavery in Israel before He could deal with it in the Gentile nations. Had the Jews treated one another as the law required, Israel would have been a testimony to the Gentile nations of the grace and kindness of the Lord. Instead, Israel failed to obey and eventually became slaves themselves, as recorded in the Book of Judges.

Even in the New Testament, you find neither Jesus nor Paul openly attacking slavery, although historians tell us there were probably 60 million slaves in the Roman Empire in that day. But Jesus and Paul brought the message of salvation *to individuals,* and it would be through saved individuals that the institution of slavery would finally be abolished. Christians are the salt of the earth and the light of the world (Matt. 5:13-16), and they make their influence felt through example and persuasion. As Alexander Maclaren wrote, "[The Gospel message] meddles directly with no political or social arrangements, but lays down principles which will profoundly affect these, and leaves them to soak into the general mind."[3]

If the early church had launched a militant crusade against slavery, it would have identified Christianity as a political movement, and this would have hindered the spreading of the Gospel in the Roman world. Since there were no democracies or popular elections in those days, the church had no vehicle for overthrowing slavery. When you consider how difficult it's been for the contemporary civil rights movement even to influence the Christian church, how much more difficult it would have been to wage such a war in the days of Caesar!

For reasons that are known only to Him, the Lord chooses to change people and society gradually, through the ministry of the Holy Spirit and the proclamation of the truth of the Word of God. While the principles of God's will are the same from age to age, we have no authority to apply to society today the laws that regulated Israel during the dispensation of the Mosaic Law.

A Jew enslaved by a Gentile (vv. 47-55) could be redeemed by a near kinsman who was willing and wealthy enough to do it. It's interesting to note that a Gentile "resident alien" in the land of Israel had to obey the Law of Moses, even though he wasn't a member of the Jewish covenant community. If the Jew was able to raise the purchase price, he could buy his freedom, and the price would be calculated according to the Year of Jubilee. The Gentile master was required to treat the

Jewish slave as a hired servant and not treat him harshly. If not redeemed, the slave and his family would be released at the Year of Jubilee.

The classic example of the law of the kinsman-redeemer is recorded in the Book of Ruth, where Boaz redeemed both Ruth and her inheritance and then married her. The Lord Jesus Christ took upon Himself sinless human flesh and became our "near kinsman" (Heb. 2:5-18), so that He might give Himself as the redemption price and set us free. Only He was qualified to do what had to be done, and He was willing to do it. Not only did He redeem us, but also He gave us a share in and made us a part of His inheritance!

It's unfortunate that the Jewish people didn't obey the laws given in this chapter, for their selfishness and greed brought ruin to the land and their economic system. The prophets rebuked the rich for exploiting the poor and stealing their houses, lands, and even their children (Isa. 3:14-15; 10:1-3; Amos 2:6-7; 5:11). The local courts ignored God's decrees; the judges, enriched by bribes, passed down decisions that favored the wealthy and crushed the poor. But God heard the cries of the poor and one day brought terrible judgment to the people of Israel.

God is concerned about how we use the resources He's given us and how we treat one another in the marketplace. Both ecology and economy are His concern, and He eventually judges those who exploit others and treat them in ways that are less than humane (Amos 1–2). The church of Jesus Christ has thrived under many kinds of political and economic systems and isn't dependent on any of them, but the church must always champion the rights of the poor and the oppressed and use every spiritual weapon to defeat the oppressors.

"A decent provision for the poor is the true test of civilization," said British writer Samuel Johnson.

"You hear, O Lord, the desire of the afflicted; You encourage them, and You listen to their cry, defending the fatherless and the oppressed, in order that man, who is of the earth, may terrify no more" (Ps. 10:17-18, NIV).

The Big Word "If"

The word "if" has been called one of the shortest and yet one of the most important words in the English language. Debating over what might have happened in world history *if* Wellington had lost at Waterloo or *if* Lee had won at Gettysburg is an exercise in futility.

When you leave the "ifs" out of Leviticus 26–27, you may miss the meaning; for "if" is used thirty-two times. The history of Israel can't be fully understood apart from the "ifs" contained in God's covenant. When it comes to Jewish history, "if" is a very big word. Three "if" phrases in chapter 26 show us the importance of the word: "If you walk in My statutes" (v. 3, NKJV); "But if you do not obey Me" (v. 14, NKJV); "But if they confess their iniquity" (v. 40, NKJV). In our relationship to the Lord, "if" carries a lot of weight.

The statutes and instructions God gave Israel in Leviticus 26 and 27 illustrate four responsibilities that every Christian believer has toward the Lord.

1. Obeying His commandments (Lev. 26:1-13)

In Leviticus 26, to obey God is to "walk in [His] statutes" (v. 3), but to disobey Him is to "walk contrary" to the Lord and despise His statutes (vv. 15, 21, 23-24, 27-28, 40-41). The word translated "contrary" means "a hostile meeting with the intention of fighting."[1]

If I'm walking one direction and God is walking another, I'm moving away from His presence; *and God isn't about to change His direction!* If I continue to walk contrary to Him, I'm going to have serious problems; for "can two walk together, except they be agreed?" (Amos 3:3) Moses gave his people four excellent reasons why they should obey the Lord.

Because of who God is (v. 1). The God of Israel, the God and Father of our Lord Jesus Christ, is the true and living God and not an idol people have manufactured. He reminded them, "I am the LORD your God." The name LORD in capital letters signifies Jehovah God, the great I AM, the self-existent One who entered into a covenant relationship with Israel and to whom the Jews said, "All that the Lord has spoken we will do" (see Ex. 19:1-8).

A.W. Tozer reminds us, "The essence of idolatry is the entertaining of thoughts about God that are unworthy of Him" *(The Knowledge of the Holy,* 11). When the Jews abandoned the worship of Jehovah for the worship of idols, or even worse, tried to worship *both* Jehovah and idols, they turned from reality to illusion, from truth to deception; and the consequences were disastrous. In spite of their promise to obey the Lord, the Jews broke the first two commandments when they turned to idols.

Because of what God did (v. 2a). The word "Sabbaths" (plural) refers to *all* the special days on the Jewish calendar and not just the seventh day of the week. We studied this calendar in chapter 9 and noted that these special days reminded the Jews of God's goodness to them. Passover memorialized Israel's deliverance from Egypt, and the Feast of Tabernacles reminded them of God's care of His people in the wilderness. Firstfruits and Pentecost were "harvest festivals" that spoke of the Lord's blessing on their labors in the field, and Tabernacles was a time of harvest joy because of the fruit God gave in the vineyard and the orchard.

Even the weekly Sabbath was a reminder that the Jews were God's special people, for the Sabbath Day was a sign between the Lord and Israel (Ex. 31:13). As they rested on the seventh day, the Jews could give thanks that they belonged to the true and living God who adopted Israel as His own special treasure. They could also give thanks that God had strengthened them to labor for another week. Whether they reviewed Jewish history from the Exodus or just meditated on God's goodness from the previous week, the Jews had plenty of reason to thank God and obey His statutes.

Because of where God dwells (v. 2b). The God of Israel dwelt in the camp of Israel! The Jews had His sacred tabernacle in the midst of the camp with the "glory cloud" hovering over it. The nations around them had man-made gods in their temples, but Israel had *the God who made them* dwelling in their midst. How could they ever think of disobeying Him when He was so near to them, condescending to live with them in their camp? To deliberately disobey God was not only a violation of His holy law, but it was also a desecration of His sanctuary. To sin was to defile the camp, which explains why unclean people were made to leave the camp.

The application to the Christian believer today is obvious. Our bodies are the sanctuary of God, and we must be careful to use them for God's glory (1 Cor. 6:15-20). The Holy Spirit of God lives in us, and we must not grieve Him by using His temple for ungodly purposes (Eph. 4:30; see vv. 17-32). If an Old Testament Jew sacrificed a pig on the altar or scattered human bones in the tabernacle courtyard, he would have been guilty of the grossest violations of God's holy law. Christians who indulge in illicit sex or who defile their imagination with evil thoughts are guilty of violations just as serious.

Because of what God promised (vv. 3-13). The people of
Israel were but children in their faith (Gal. 4:1-7), and you
teach children primarily through rewards and punishments.
You can't give children lectures on ethics and expect them to
understand, but you can promise to reward them if they obey
and punish them if they disobey. This approach will protect
them from harming themselves, and it will give them time to
grow older and better understand *why* obedience is the key to
a happy life. Children must gradually learn that both commandments and punishments are expressions of love for their
own good.

Moses later expanded on this "covenant of blessing"
(Deut. 28–30). It was God's "lease" for the people to help
them enjoy and maintain possession of the land that He
promised to give them. They *owned* the land because of
God's promises to Abraham (Gen. 12:1-3; 13:14-17), but they
couldn't *enjoy* the land unless they obeyed the laws God gave
to Moses. Unfortunately, they disobeyed the law, ceased to
enjoy the land, and eventually were taken from the land to
suffer exile in Babylon.

As children of God, we already have everything we need
for "life and godliness" (2 Peter 1:3), because we now possess "every spiritual blessing in Christ" (Eph. 1:3, NIV). But
to possess these blessings is one thing; to enjoy them is
quite something else. As we trust God's promises and obey
His commandments, we draw upon our spiritual inheritance
and are able to walk successfully and serve effectively. Like
the nation of Israel in Canaan, we have battles to fight and
work to do; but as we walk in obedience to the Lord, He
enables us to overcome the enemy, claim the land, and enjoy
its blessings.

To begin with, God promised them *rain and fruitful harvests (Lev. 26:3-5, 10).* An agricultural nation, Israel depended
on the "latter rain" in the spring and the "former rain" in the

autumn to provide water for their crops and to meet their domestic needs. One reason Baal worship ensnared the Israelites is because Baal was the Canaanite storm god. If the Jews needed rain, they sometimes turned to Baal for help instead of turning to Jehovah. If God wanted to discipline His people, He would often withhold the rain, as He did in the days of Elijah (1 Kings 17–18).

The Lord also promised them *peace and safety in their land (Lev. 26:5-8).* They could go to bed without fear of either animals or enemies invading their land. If the enemy did invade, the Jewish armies would soon chase them out; and one Jewish soldier would be worth twenty to a hundred of the enemy soldiers! Other nations depended for safety on large armies and supplies of horses and chariots, but Israel's victory came through faith in the Lord and obedience to His Word. "Some trust in chariots, and some in horses: but we will remember the name of the Lord our God" (Ps. 20:7).

If Israel obeyed His law, God promised to *multiply their population (Lev. 26:9).* Unlike some today who abort babies and frown upon large families, the Jews wanted many children and considered large families a blessing from God (Gen. 17:6; Deut. 7:13-14; Pss. 127–128). New generations were needed to maintain the economy, to help sustain the clans and tribes, and to protect the nation. A decimated population was a judgment from the Lord.

The presence of the Lord (Lev. 26:11-12) was the greatest blessing promised, because every other blessing depends on it. What other nation had the sanctuary of the living God in their midst and their God walking among them? (Rom. 9:1-5) How tragic that Israel's disobedience turned the temple into a den of thieves (Jer. 7:11), forcing the Lord to destroy the temple and send His people into exile. When we lose the sense of the Lord's presence and the privilege it is to serve Him, then we begin to despise His Word and disobey His commandments.

Nine times in Leviticus we find the Lord reminding His people that He had delivered them out from Egypt and therefore deserved their obedience (Lev. 11:45; 19:36; 22:33; 23:43; 25:38, 42, 55; 26:13, 45). In Deuteronomy, Moses emphasized that their love for the Lord should motivate their obedience because of all He had done for them.

It must be pointed out that this covenant of blessing was given only to Israel and should not be applied to the church today. God certainly blesses those who obey Him, but His blessing isn't always health, wealth, and success. Some of the greatest heroes of faith suffered because of their obedience and never experienced miracles of deliverance or provision from the Lord (Heb. 11:36-40). Millions of Christians have been allowed to fall into the hands of their enemies and be martyred for their faith. This covenant related only to Israel in their land and was God's way of teaching them faithfulness and obedience.

Some of the "success preachers" today like to claim these covenant "blessings" for the church but prefer to apply the judgments to somebody else! If this covenant applies to God's children today, then we should be experiencing the judgments whenever we disobey Him. However, experience shows us that more than one compromising believer is successful, healthy, and wealthy, while many of God's faithful children are going through trials and difficulties (see Ps. 73).

2. Submitting to His chastisements (Lev. 26:14-39)

"For whom the Lord loves He chastens, and scourges every son whom He receives" (Heb. 12:6, NKJV; see Prov. 3:11-12). Israel's special relationship to Jehovah brought with it the obligation to obey His voice and glorify His name. "You only have I known [chosen] of all the families of the earth: therefore I will punish you for all your iniquities" (Amos 3:2). Privilege brings with it responsibility, and no nation has enjoyed more spiritual privileges from the Lord than the nation of Israel.

Six periods of chastisement are described (Lev. 26:16-17, 18-20, 21-22, 23-26, 27-31 and 32-39), the last one being the most severe. In the first five, Jehovah punishes the people *in their own land;* but in the sixth judgment, they're taken *out of the land* and dispersed among the nations. Some of the chastisements are repeated from period to period, but they can be summarized as follows: distress and terror; disease; drought and famine; defeat before their enemies; death from war, animals, and plagues; destruction of the cities and nation; dispersement and exile among the Gentile nations. Moses later expanded on these chastisements (Deut. 28:15ff). How sad that innocent children would have to suffer for the sins of their parents (Lev. 26:22, 29).

The phrase "I will punish you seven times more," repeated four times in these warnings (vv. 18, 21, 24, 28), means "a complete punishment," since seven is the Hebrew number signifying completeness. Each period of chastisement would be full and complete, with nothing lacking; and the next period would be more severe than the previous one.

Verses 16-17. "Sudden terror" means confusion of mind, the kind of terror you feel when you can't control what's going on. "Consumption" would describe diseases that slowly wasted the body, like tuberculosis. During the Book of Judges, the Gentile nations invaded Israel at harvest time and took their crops. If the Israelites had obeyed, God's face would have "[shone] upon them" (Num. 6:22-27); but their disobedience made Him turn His face away from them (compare Lev. 26:17 with Prov. 28:1).

Verses 18-20. God's aim was to "break down [their] stubborn pride" (v. 19, NIV). The rains would cease and the ground would become so hard that the seed wouldn't germinate. There would be great toil but no harvests (Amos 4:6-

13). You would think that all this suffering would bring the nation to its knees in repentance, but they refused to repent. It will be that way in the end times when God sends judgment upon the whole world (Rev. 16, especially vv. 9 and 11).

Verses 21-22. One judgment is named here: the invasion of wild beasts that would kill cattle and humans, especially the children. Imagine the terror that would prevail in a nation if hungry beasts were on the prowl! If only for the sake of their children, you would think the adults would repent and turn to God.

Verses 23-26. Warfare, famine, and plague usually go together. When people are crowded into a walled city, hemmed in by the enemy, they run out of food and become ill, and terrible plagues begin to spread (see Ezek. 5).

Verses 27-31. Famine causes people to do things that are inhuman, such as killing and eating their own children (see 2 Kings 6:29, Jer. 19:9; Lam. 4:10). The enemy armies would destroy the idolatrous shrines the Jews had built and throw the dead bodies of the Jews onto their idols which could not save them. Leviticus 26:31 suggests that the people would try to revive their worship of Jehovah, but it would be too late. Their cities and sanctuaries would all be leveled to the ground.

Verses 32-39. This section describes the climax of God's chastisements, made necessary because of the hardness of His people's hearts. Up to this point, He had chastened the people *in* their land, but now He removes them *from* the land. In 722 B.C., the Assyrians took captive the Northern Kingdom of Israel; and then in 605 B.C., the Babylonians began their capture of the Southern Kingdom of Judah. The seventy years of Babylonian Captivity left the land to rest and "enjoy her sabbaths" (vv. 34-35, 43; 2 Chron. 36:21; Jer. 25:11).

The Lord mercifully brought a remnant of Jews back to the

land, but the kingdom never regained its former power or glory. Except for short periods of freedom, such as under the Maccabees, the Jews were always under the control of some foreign power. Their ultimate dispersion was after A.D. 70, when the Roman armies invaded and took Jerusalem captive. The siege of Jerusalem more than fulfilled the prophecies in Leviticus 26:22 and 29.

3. Trusting His covenant (Lev. 26:40-46)

Even in the worst situations, however, there is always hope; for the Lord is "merciful and gracious, long-suffering, and abundant in goodness and truth, keeping mercy for thousands, forgiving iniquity and transgression and sin" (Ex. 34:6-7). His covenant with His people never changes; and if we confess our sins and repent, He will forgive and restore (Lev. 26:40; 1 Kings 8:33-34; Neh. 9:2; 1 John 1:9). Whether in blessing, chastening, or forgiving, God always keeps His covenant and is true to His Word.

God may punish His people, but He will never reject them or cast them away (Rom. 11). In fact, one reason for His chastening is to bring His erring people back into His arms of love, where He can enjoy them and bless them once again (Heb. 12:1-13). God's people may forget His law, but God remembers His covenant. He also remembers the land, because it belongs to Him (Lev. 25:23).

There will be a future regathering of Israel to their land prior to the coming of Christ to the earth to establish His promised kingdom. (See the discussion on the Feast of Trumpets in chap. 9 of this book.) God gave the land to Abraham and his descendants, and He will not go back on His Word.

The cause of Israel's rebellion was "uncircumcised hearts," that is, hearts that had never been changed by the Lord (26:41). The Jews boasted that they were circumcised in body, but that wasn't enough to save them (Matt. 3:7-12). The mark on the body was the outward seal of the covenant, but it took more than that to change the heart (see Deut. 10:16; 30:6; Jer. 4:4; 9:25; Rom. 2:29).

When we disobey the Lord, the enemy accuses us and wants us to believe there's no hope because God is through with us (2 Cor. 2:1-11). "If we are faithless, He will remain faithful, for He cannot disown Himself" (2 Tim. 2:13, NIV). King Solomon pointed out the promise of forgiveness when he dedicated the temple (1 Kings 8:31-53), and it was that promise that Jonah claimed when he repented of his sins (Jonah 2:7).

The promise of forgiveness in 1 John 1:9 should never be used as an excuse for sin, but it is certainly a wonderful encouragement to God's people when they have sinned. God's faithfulness to His Word and to His covenant is a great assurance to the believer that "there is forgiveness with You, that You may be feared" (Ps. 130:4, NKJV). Since the Word never changes and God's character never changes, we have every encouragement to come to Him and make a new beginning.

4. Keeping our commitments to God (Lev. 27:1-34)

It seems strange that this book should end with a chapter on vows rather than with an account of a special demonstration of God's glory and holiness. But our promises to God must be as inviolable as His covenant with us. "Do not be rash with your mouth, and let not your heart utter anything hastily before God" (Ecc. 5:2, NKJV). "It is a snare for a man to devote rashly something as holy, and afterward to reconsider his vows" (Prov. 20:25, NKJV).

The principle behind the regulations in this chapter is that of substituting money for something given in dedication to God, a person, an animal, or a piece of property, and giving that money to the priests for the upkeep of the sanctuary. The priest would evaluate the gift according to the rules laid down in this chapter. By giving money in exchange for the gift, the worshiper was "redeeming" the gift but still fulfilling the vow. These vows were strictly voluntary and were expressions of the worshiper's gratitude to God for His blessing.

The redeemable things (vv. 1-25). They started with the dedication of persons (vv. 1-8). A worshiper might dedicate himself to the Lord or bring a member of the family or a servant to serve the Lord for life at the sanctuary. However, since there were plenty of Levites, and since they were especially set apart for sanctuary service, it was expected that the person given would be redeemed with money, and the money given to the priests for the ministry of the sanctuary. In the case of Samuel (1 Sam. 1–2), the lad was actually given to the high priest and trained to serve in the tabernacle. Children could be redeemed or, like Samuel, they could go into service when they became older.

The amount of money assigned to each age bracket and sex had nothing to do with the worth of the individual as a person. Everyone was precious to the Lord. The key idea was how much work they would have been able to do. A shekel was the equivalent of a month's income for a worker, although we don't know how much buying power it had. Thus a male from twenty to sixty was evaluated at about four years' income. Put that into modern economic equivalents, and you will rightly conclude that people didn't rush into making these vows! It would indeed be a costly thing to pay four years' income to fulfill a vow to the Lord.

Animals could also be dedicated and then redeemed (Lev. 27:9-13). Every animal dedicated to the Lord was considered holy (vv. 9-10), which meant it was set apart ("sanctified") and belonged to the Lord. If the donor wanted to substitute an inferior beast, *both* animals then belonged to the Lord! (v. 10) This was one of the sins of the priests in Malachi's day (Mal. 1:13-14). In the case of animals, the donor had to add 20 percent to the priest's evaluation.

Property could also be dedicated and redeemed (Lev. 27:14-25), but the owner had to add 20 percent to the evaluation when he gave the redemption money to the priest. A field was evaluated on the basis of its yield and the proximity to the Year of Jubilee. If for some reason the owner sold the land after devoting it to the Lord, he was penalized by losing it at the Year of Jubilee, when it would be given to the priests and could never be redeemed. When we make promises to the Lord, we had better keep them.

The unredeemable things (vv. 26-34). There are three: the firstborn of the beasts, anything God put under a ban, and the required tithes.

The firstlings of the beasts (vv. 26-27) were set apart for the Lord at the first Passover (Ex. 13:2; see 34:19-20). These animals took the place of the firstborn of Israel whom the blood of the lamb redeemed from judgment. These animals could not be redeemed. But if the animal was "unclean," which probably means blemished in some way, the donor could redeem it by paying the evaluated price and adding 20 percent. (No blemished animal would be put on the altar, and certainly a priest could never accept an animal listed as "unclean.")

Things "devoted" to the Lord (vv. 28-29) would be things that God had set aside for Himself, such as the spoils of war at Jericho (Josh. 6:17-19; 7:11-15). The phrase "accursed thing" in the KJV doesn't mean that God cursed these things but that He put them under a ban so that they wholly belonged to Him. King Saul broke this law when he tried to give to God that which He had already banned, that is, the Amalekites and all their wealth (1 Sam. 15).

145

The tithes of the produce (vv. 30-33) had already been set apart for the Lord and couldn't be used any other way. It appears that the Jews paid three tithes: a tithe to the Levites, who in turn tithed it to the priests (Num. 18:21-32); a tithe that was brought to the sanctuary and eaten "before the Lord" (Deut. 14:22-27); and a tithe every three years for the poor (vv. 28-29). No farmer could keep the Lord's tithe and redeem it with money. It had to be given as the Lord directed.

The major lesson of this chapter is that God expects us to keep our commitments to Him and be honest in all our dealings with Him. We must not try to negotiate "a better deal" or to escape responsibilities. It's good to give money to the Lord, but giving money isn't always an acceptable way to express our devotion to God. That money might be a substitute for the service we ought to be rendering to the Lord.

What Samuel said to King Saul needs to be heard today: "Behold, to obey is better than sacrifice, and to hearken than the fat of rams" (1 Sam. 15:22).

Finally, we need to remember that Jesus Christ paid with His own life the redemption price for sinners, *and we weren't worth it.* He redeemed us not with silver and gold but with His own precious blood (1 Peter 1:18-19). Any sacrifice we make for Him is nothing compared to the sacrifice He made for us.

A SUMMARY

Learning from Leviticus

The fact that God devoted an entire book of the Bible to the subject of holiness would indicate that it's an *important* subject, one that we dare not ignore. There were many fascinating details in this book that we weren't able to study, but the main lessons stand out clearly. Let's summarize a few of these lessons and make some practical applications to our Christian life today.

1. Our God is a holy God

Whenever we minimize the holiness of God, we're in danger of minimizing human sinfulness, and the combination of these two errors results in the minimizing of the cross of Jesus Christ. If we want to preach the Gospel, we must have a holy God who hates sin and has done something about it at great cost to Himself. "It is because God is holy, as well as loving, that the atonement is provided," wrote theologian Carl F.H. Henry.[1]

God's holiness means His complete "apartness" from anything that is sinful. He is *different* from that which is common; He is *separate* from that which is defiling. But God's holiness isn't a static thing, like a block of pure ice. His holiness is active and alive, a "sea of glass mingled with fire" (Rev. 15:2). Everything about God is holy: His wisdom, His power, His judgments, and even His love. If His love were not a holy love, He would never have sent His only Son to die for the sins of the world and meet the just demands of His own nature and His own holy law.

I may be wrong, but I sense that many of God's people today have lost the awesome sense of the holiness of God. Why?

For one thing, we don't emphasize holiness in our churches. Like the campfire meeting of a Boy Scout troop, our "worship" services are spritely and joyful but totally lacking in the important emphasis on the holiness of God. Our preaching is people-centered, trying to "scratch people where they itch," instead of pointing them to the holy God, who deserves their worship and obedience. People who get caught up in the greatness and holiness of God don't worry much about where they itch.

The absence of church discipline and high standards of Christian conduct indicates that we don't take holiness too seriously. In our promotion, we try to "sell" the church to the world by conveying the unbiblical idea that Christianity is "fun" and every pagan ought to join the club and start living on the sunny side of the street. I once heard a pastor say in his announcements, "Be sure to be at the service this evening. We're going to have a fun time." I thought of the words of James, written to worldly believers: "Lament and mourn and weep! Let your laughter be turned to mourning and your joy to gloom" (James 4:9, NKJV).

I can't conceive of Moses and the elders "having fun" on Mt. Sinai as they beheld the glory of God, or Isaiah reporting that he had a "fun time" in the temple when he saw "the Lord . . . high and lifted up" (Isa. 6:1). Nobody enjoys good humor and healthy laughter more than I do, but as I contemplate my sinfulness and God's holiness, I want to join Job, Isaiah, Peter, and John and fall on my face in reverence and godly fear.

2. God wants His people to be holy

Eight times in Scripture, God said, "Be holy, for I am holy." Since God's commandments are God's enablements, this commandment assures us that it's possible to live a holy life. What health is to the body, holiness is to the soul; and the Great Physician can give us the spiritual health and wholeness that we need.

God wanted His people Israel to be "an holy nation" (Ex. 19:6), and this high calling applies to Christians today (1 Peter 2:9). Whatever else the church may be known for today—buildings, budgets, crowds, busy schedules—it certainly isn't known for its holiness. *How many Christians do you know about whom you could honestly say, "He is a man of God" or "She is a woman of God"?* How many "Christian celebrities" qualify?

Israel failed to be a holy nation and therefore failed to give the witness to the world that God wanted them to give. Not only did *Israel* suffer for her sins, but also *the pagan world* suffered by not seeing in Israel the difference it makes when you belong to a holy God. The church emphasizes verbal witness but neglects godly character and conduct, and both are important. Jesus didn't say, "Ye are the lips of the world," but "Ye are the light of the world." He didn't say, "Ye are the sermons of the earth," but "Ye are the salt of the earth." A holy life dispels darkness and repels decay.

3. Holiness begins at the altar

The Book of Leviticus doesn't begin with a prayer meeting, a praise service, or a sharing meeting. It begins at the altar where innocent sacrifices shed their blood for guilty sinners.

It begins with the description of five sacrifices, all of which point to the Lord Jesus Christ and His work on the cross.

The first step toward holiness is the admission of my own sin and the recognition of Christ as my only Savior and Redeemer from sin. If I think I'm going to become holy because of my sincere resolutions, my religious habits, or my theological knowledge, I'm heading for certain failure. True, we need spiritual knowledge, and we ought to resolve to cultivate godly habits; but apart from the sacrifice of Jesus Christ, all these good things are useless if not harmful.

The cross reveals God's hatred of sin. *Our sins killed His only Son.* How can I be neutral or even friendly toward that which caused the Son of God to suffer and die? Unless I learn to detest sin, I'll never be able to cultivate holiness.

But the cross also reveals the power of God to conquer sin. The blood of Christ cleanses us (1 John 1:7, 9), brings us near to God (Eph. 2:13), and purges us from sin (Heb. 9:14). By accepting His finished work and our sanctified position in Him (13:12), we take that first step toward living a holy life.

4. Holiness involves obedience and discipline

It wasn't enough for the Jewish worshiper to bring a sacrifice to the altar and go away knowing that his or her sins had been forgiven. That worshiper also had to obey the rules and regulations that the Lord gave His people concerning what was clean and what was unclean. In other words, our holy God has the right to tell us what's right and what's wrong.

Believers today don't pay attention to the Jewish dietary laws, but we should heed what they illustrate: There are some things in this world that must not get into our system because God disapproves of them. I'm not afraid to touch a dead body or pick up a bone, but I must be careful "to keep [myself] unspotted from the world" (James 1:27). Christian liberty isn't license to participate in things that aren't good for us.

I applaud the current emphasis on Bible study among Christians and rejoice at the many excellent tools that are available. But it isn't enough to read and study the Bible. We're supposed to "keep His commandments, and do those things that are pleasing in His sight" (1 John 3:22). *Disciplined obedience is an important part of holy living.* It's much easier to discuss and debate the Bible than it is to demonstrate its truths in our everyday lives.

The Old Testament Jews had to walk carefully to keep from being defiled (Eph. 5:15). They had to incorporate God's standards of holiness into every aspect of their daily lives: the clothes they wore, the food they ate, the things they touched, the people with whom they fellowshipped. Husbands and wives had to put their most intimate experiences under the discipline of the Word of God. There was no such thing as "secular" and "sacred" to the Old Testament saint, for everything in life belonged to God.

Believers today think they're spiritual if they attend church once a week and read from a devotional book the other six days. It's only when God's holiness increasingly begins to touch *every area of our lives* that we can say we're starting to make progress in being holy.

5. Holiness must be from God and be genuine
We must beware of "false zeal." God killed Nadab and Abihu, the sons of Aaron, because they brought "false fire" and false zeal into the sanctuary, violating the holy law of God. God doesn't do that today; but if He did, not very many saints would be left. It's likely that the two priests were under the influence of alcohol, which brings to mind Paul's admonition that we not be drunk with wine but be filled with the Spirit (Eph. 5:18).

Refined human nature can imitate spirituality but never duplicate it. Sentimental religious feelings are no guarantee that we're pleasing God, and the absence of them doesn't mean we're failing God. I'm grateful for the renewed emphasis in the church on worship and praise, but we must be careful that our "fire" is ignited by the Holy Spirit from God's altar and not by the flesh or even demonic forces. Satan is a deceiver, and we must be careful to detect and reject his counterfeits.

6. Holiness involves priestly mediation

The Old Testament Jew, not born in the tribe of Levi, was banned from the sacred courts of the tabernacle. He had to come to God by means of the mediation of the priests. In the New Testament church, all of God's people are priests; *but we must come to God through Jesus Christ, our mediating High Priest in heaven* (1 Peter 2:5).

There can be no growth in holiness apart from fellowship with Jesus Christ. He finished the work of our salvation when He died and arose again on earth, but He now carries on the "unfinished work" of our sanctification as He intercedes in heaven. This is one of the major themes of the Book of Hebrews. He wants to "make you perfect in every good work to do His will, working in you that which is wellpleasing in His sight, through Jesus Christ" (Heb. 13:21).

Unlike the Old Testament believers, God's people today can enter into His very presence (the holy of holies) and fellowship with Him (10:19-22). Through Jesus Christ, we have access to the throne of grace to "obtain mercy, and find grace to help in time of need" (4:16). Unless we "take time to be holy" and commune with God, we will never grow in holiness or likeness to Jesus Christ.

7. Lack of holiness affects our land

We tend to think of sin as an individual activity that affects only the sinner, but this isn't true. Moses made it clear that the sins of the people affected the land God had given them, and that the land would "vomit them out" if they persisted in their rebellion.

Idolatry and sexual immorality are the two sins that God especially singled out as polluting the land. "Do not defile yourselves in any of these ways, because this is how the nations that I am going to drive out before you became defiled. Even the land was defiled; so I punished it for its sin, and the land vomited out its inhabitants" (Lev. 18:24-25, NIV).

Although we should do all we can to uphold holy standards, the church doesn't have the authority to impose God's laws on the unsaved citizens of the land. But what should we do when *the people in the church, who profess to know God, don't practice these standards themselves?* When the church becomes like the world, it will have no influence to change the world.

Idolatry and immorality are not only acceptable in today's society, but they are also approved and promoted. Novels, movies, and TV programs exhibit and exalt sexual immorality to the point where it has become an important part of today's entertainment. Sins that ought to send us to our knees weeping are now acceptable recreation. We expect this kind of godless living from the people of the world, but we don't expect it from the people of God; and yet idolatry and immorality have invaded the church.

Judgment is coming, and it will begin "at the house of God" (1 Peter 4:17).

8. Holiness isn't a private affair

The Old Testament believer was part of a worshiping community; he or she didn't try to "go it alone." The priests were the overseers of the spiritual life of the nation; the Levites assisted them; and each member of the nation had a part to play in the ongoing battle against sin and the world.

One of the dangerous tendencies in Christendom today is

the emphasis on "individual Christianity," as though each believer is a "Lone Ranger" and doesn't need anybody else to assist him or her in the quest for holiness. Of course, we need individual and personal daily devotional times with the Lord, but it mustn't end there. We also need the help of our spiritual leaders and other believers in the church, and they need us.

The restful Sabbath Day gave parents opportunity to teach the Word to their children, and each Passover was another opportunity to review God's mercy toward His people. The other feasts brought the community together, either to repent or rejoice. When we forsake "the assembling of ourselves together" (Heb. 10:25), we rob ourselves of the blessings God gives to those who are a vital part of a worshiping fellowship.

9. Holiness glorifies the Lord

Since only God can make a person holy, a godly life is a trophy of His grace and a tribute to His power. Teachers can take credit for instructing us, pastors for mentoring us, and friends for encouraging us, but only God gets the glory when people see Christ reproduced in us.

We may not see the changes taking place, but God can see them, and so can others. The important thing isn't that we measure ourselves the way we measure the growth of our children, but that we keep yielding ourselves and letting Him be glorified in all that we are and do.

10. Holiness means living to please God alone

If a Jew, walking alone in a field, accidentally became unclean, he could do one of two things. He could stay outside the camp and take the necessary steps for cleansing, or he could return to the camp, do nothing about it, and remain defiled. Nobody would know the difference, but he would be "toxic" and secretly defiling everything and everyone he touched; *and the Lord would know all about it.* Unless he obeyed the regulations given in God's law and became clean again, he would be living a lie, doing a great deal of damage and inviting the discipline of God.

One of the principles Jesus stressed in the Sermon on the Mount is that we live our lives before the eyes of God, to please Him alone, and not before the eyes of people in order to impress them (Matt. 6:1-18). There are times when what we do is misunderstood by our friends on earth but fully understood and approved by our Father in heaven. In other words, Jesus wants us to concentrate on building character and not just building a religious reputation.

It makes no difference how loudly our friends applaud if God is displeased with us. "Everything is uncovered and laid bare before the eyes of Him to whom we must give account" (Heb. 4:13, NIV), so it's futile to try to hide. According to 1 John 1:5-10, once we start lying to others (v. 6), we'll soon start lying to ourselves (v. 8); and the result will be trying to lie to God (v. 10). This leads to a gradual deterioration of character that brings collapse and shame. We seek to live a holy life, not so that we can be recognized as "holy people," but in order to please a holy God. We live before Him openly and sincerely, hiding nothing, fearing nothing.

For several years, I've had a plaque on the wall of my study containing this quotation from A.W. Tozer: "To know God is at once the easiest and the most difficult thing in the world."

Knowing God and becoming more like Him is the easiest thing in the world because God is for us and gives us all the help we want as we seek to attain the goal. But it's the hardest thing because almost everything within us and around us fights against us, and we have to exercise a holy determination to run the race and keep our eyes on the Lord (Heb. 12:1-3).

But it can be done; otherwise, God would never have said eight times in His Word, "Be holy, for I am holy!"

His commandment is the promise of His enablement.

Be holy!

ENDNOTES

Preface
1. A.W. Tozer, *The Price of Neglect* (Camp Hill, Pa.: Christian Publications, 1991), 24.

Chapter 1
1. Leviticus 11:44-45; 19:2; 20:7, 26; 21:8; 1 Peter 1:15-16.
2. Augustus H. Strong, *Systematic Theology* (Philadelphia: The Judson Press, 12th edition, 1949), 271.
3. There are three aspects of sanctification that should be noted: positional, practical, and perfect. Positional sanctification means that the believer is once-and-for-all set apart for God (1 Cor. 1:2; 6:9-11; Heb. 10:10). Practical sanctification is the process by which the believer daily becomes more like Christ (John 17:17; 2 Cor. 3:18; 7:1). Perfect sanctification will be our experience when we see Christ in glory (1 John 3:2). One of the "birthmarks" of a true believer is a hatred for sin and a desire to become more like Jesus Christ (1 John 2:29; 3:9; 5:4-5). We are saved to become holy in Christ (Eph. 1:4; 5:27; Col. 1:22).

Chapter 2
1. Hebrews 10:5-8 refers to all six of the levitical sacrifices and states that they are fulfilled in Jesus Christ. "Sacrifice" (v. 5) refers to any animal sacrifice, which would include the peace (fellowship) offering, burnt offering, sin offering, and trespass (guilt) offering. "Offering" (v. 5) refers to the meal and drink offerings. The burnt offering and sin offering are specifically named in verses 6 and 8.
2. Even the poorest in the nation could bring a sacrifice to God. When Mary and Joseph dedicated the Baby Jesus, they brought birds instead of animals (Luke 2:21-24; see Lev. 12:8; 2 Cor. 8:9).
3. The Hebrew word translated "lay in order" (vv. 7-8, 12) can be

found in the prayer in Psalm 5:3 ("I lay my requests before You," NIV). Like the sacrifices on the altar, our prayers should be orderly and "on fire" before God. Prayer is also compared to the burning of incense on the golden altar (141:2).

4. When Paul admonished Timothy to "stir up the gift of God" (2 Tim. 1:6), he used a Greek word that literally means "again — life — fire" and was saying "fan the fire into life again." As God's priests, believers today must keep the fire burning on the altar of their hearts and not become lukewarm (Rev. 3:15-16) or cold (Matt. 24:12).

5. In seventeenth-century England, when the KJV was translated, the word "meat" meant any kind of food, including grain; and so the translators called this "the meat offering," even though no "meat" (animal flesh) was involved. It should be called the "grain offering," "meal offering," or "cereal offering."

6. However, see Leviticus 5:11-13, where the meal offering could be presented by poor people unable to afford an animal; and God said He would forgive their sins. But keep in mind that since the meal was placed on the altar on which the daily burnt offering had been sacrificed (Ex. 29:38-42), there was "the shedding of blood."

7. The "whole rump" mentioned in 3:9 and 7:3 refers to "the entire fat tail" of the sheep, which could weigh as much as fifteen pounds. It was considered one of the most valuable parts of the animal, and it was given entirely to the Lord.

8. The familiar adage "Ignorance is no excuse in the sight of the law" is an adaptation of what the English jurist John Selden (1584–1654) wrote: "Ignorance of the law excuses no man; not that all men know the law, but because 'tis an excuse every man will plead, and no man can tell how to confute him." If we define "sin" as "a violation of the *known* law of God," then we're saying that the dumber we are, the holier we should be; and this isn't so. The Bible urges us to grow in knowledge that we might grow in grace (John 7:17; 2 Peter 3:18). Our exalted High Priest understands us and can help us in our ignorance (Heb. 5:2; 9:7).

9. The translation of Leviticus 5:6 in the KJV gives the impression that Leviticus 5:1-13 is about the trespass offering, when actually it

dealt with the sin offering. The trespass offering was a ram and not a female lamb or goat (5:16, 18; 6:6); the trespass offering included a fine, which is not mentioned here; and verses 5-9 and 11-12 clearly call this sacrifice a sin offering.

Chapter 3
1. The words mean "lights [or curses] and perfections," and the general feeling among interpreters is that the Urim and Thummim were "holy lots" that were cast to determine the will of God (Num. 27:21; 1 Sam. 28:6; 30:7-8).
2. Disobedience put the priests in danger of death (see Ex. 28:35, 43; 30:20-21; Lev. 16:2; Num. 4:15, 19-20). With great privileges come great responsibilities.
3. C.H. Mackintosh, *Notes on Leviticus* (Neptune, N.J.: Loizeaux, 1948), 175–76.

Chapter 4
1. See John Wesley's Sermon 93 "On Dress." The phrase "next to" means "immediately following." When people become believers, their faith ought to make a difference in the way they care for themselves.
2. According to Romans 14–15 and 1 Corinthians 8–10, Paul discussed the matter of abusing this freedom and thus offending a Christian with a weak conscience who hasn't yet grasped the meaning of freedom in Christ. We willingly lay aside our privileges, not to lose our freedom, but to help the weaker believer gain freedom. We don't want to keep people "babies" who ought to grow, but we must minister to them in love. You can't force maturity. Of course, it is foolish to eat any food that makes a person ill or that harms the believer's body, which is the temple of the Spirit of God (1 Cor. 6:19-20).
3. For an interesting study of this topic by a Christian medical doctor, see chapter 8 of *None of These Diseases* by S.I. McMillen (Revell, revised edition, 1984). See also the *New England Journal of Medicine* for May 3, 1990 (vol. 322, no. 18), 1308–15.
4. R.K. Harrison, *Leviticus, Tyndale Old Testament Commentary series* (Downers Grove, Ill.: InterVarsity, 1980), 134.

Chapter 5

1. Anybody looking forward to the "company" in hell needs to learn who they are. "But the cowardly, unbelieving, abominable, murderers, sexually immoral, sorcerers, idolaters, and all liars shall have their part in the lake which burns with fire and brimstone" (Rev. 21:8, NKJV). "But outside [the heavenly city] are dogs and sorcerers and sexually immoral and murderers and idolaters, and whoever loves and practices a lie" (22:15, NKJV). Contrast that crowd with the company the children of God will have in heaven (Heb. 12:22-24).

2. The number seven shows up frequently in Jewish ceremonies. It symbolizes completeness and fullness. The number eight suggests a new beginning.

3. It's worth noting that God doesn't put the anointing oil on man's flesh but on the blood. The Holy Spirit goes only where the blood has been applied.

4. The priest followed a similar ritual when he cleansed the house infected with mildew or fungus (Lev. 14:49-53).

5. It's likely that this law also applied to a man's uncleanness from a nocturnal emission (Lev. 22:4; Deut. 23:10-11). The mark of the covenant was on the male member, and God had every right to give laws concerning it.

6. The rabbis taught that verse 24 did not refer to a husband willfully forcing himself on his wife, but to the possibility of the wife's period beginning while they were engaged in intercourse. They couldn't believe that a Jewish man would deliberately defile himself and disobey God just for pleasure.

Chapter 6

1. Israel began her *religious* year with Passover (Ex. 12:1-2) and her *civil* year with the Feast of Trumpets (Lev. 23:23-25). Unlike our modern New Year's Day, Rosh Hashanah for the Jews is a day of fasting, confession, worship, and prayer. We would do well to follow their example instead of the example of the world.

2. John R.W. Stott, *The Cross of Christ* (Downer's Grove, Ill.: InterVarsity, 1986), 159.

ENDNOTES

3. Tyndale used this first in his translation of the Pentateuch, "the goote on which the lotte fell to scape" (Lev. 16:10). Today, a scape-goat is a person who gets blamed for something he or she didn't do, or who willingly takes the blame in order to spare somebody else.

Chapter 7

1. Believers today aren't under the Law of Moses (Rom. 6:14; 7:4; Gal. 2:19), but this doesn't mean we're allowed to be lawless. As we walk in the power of the Spirit, the righteousness demanded by the law is fulfilled in us (Rom. 8:1-4). The old nature knows no law, but the new nature needs no law. The law reveals the holiness of God, the awfulness of sin, and the great need we have for God's grace if we are going to please Him.

2. See chapter 3 of *The Apostolic Preaching of the Cross* by Leon Morris (Grand Rapids: Eerdmans, 1955).

3. Since God is the author of divine law, every disobedience is an offense against Him, even if committed against people or things (Ps. 51:4). However, some offenses are more directly related to our relationship with God, people, or things. The classification is merely a convenience, not a theological statement.

4. We sometimes hear people calling Sunday "the Christian Sab-bath," but there's no warrant in Scripture for this term. The Sab-bath is the seventh day and speaks of rest after works. Sunday is the Lord's Day, the first day of the week, the day of resurrection, and speaks of rest before works. The Sabbath belongs to the old creation; the Lord's Day to the new creation.

Chapter 8

1. Even though our Lord's priesthood belongs to the order of Mel-chizedek and not the order of Aaron (Heb. 7–9), there's still a sense in which Aaron and his sons delineate the ministry of the great High Priest who was to come. For this reason alone, they should want to be their best and do their best.

2. Aaron wasn't permitted to mourn the deaths of Nadab and Abihu, probably because they died from a judgment from God (Lev. 10:1); and Ezekiel the prophet, who was also a priest, wasn't al-lowed to lament the death of his wife (Ezek. 24:15-18). His behavior

was a sign to the people, and it gave him an opportunity to preach.
3. See Ralph Turnbull's classic book *A Minister's Obstacles* (Grand Rapids: Baker Book House, 1972), 9.

Chapter 9
1. The Spirit baptized Jewish believers into the church at Pentecost and Gentile believers in the home of Cornelius (Acts 10). Thus the imagery of the two loaves was fulfilled.
2. In calling Israel a "sinful people," I don't mean to imply that they're more sinful than the Gentile nations or even the professing church. At the Judgment Seat of Christ, the Lord will deal with the "spots and wrinkles" of His church; and it will be a serious and solemn hour. But to whom much is given, much shall be required; and Israel has been a nation especially blessed of the Lord.

Chapter 10
1. Students disagree over how long the seven lamps on the lampstand burned. Was it day and night or just from sundown to dawn? Since the sun's rays couldn't shine through the tabernacle boards in the frame, the veil at the front, or the coverings of animal skins and fabric, the priests must have needed light in the holy of holies all day long. The high priest trimmed the wicks each morning and evening, checked the oil supply, and made sure the lamps would keep burning continuously (see Ex. 30:7-8).
2. Timothy had a believing Jewish mother and an unbelieving Greek father, and he turned out well (Acts 16:1-2; 2 Tim. 1:5). Thus a mixed marriage, while not biblical (2 Cor. 6:14-18), need not automatically condemn the children to failure. However, both Timothy's mother and grandmother taught him the Scriptures from his childhood, and this helped make a difference. Again, we aren't told where Timothy's father was. Perhaps he was dead or had deserted the family and therefore had no influence on his son.
3. In the Sermon on the Mount, Jesus dealt with blasphemy and revenge (Matt. 5:33-48), thus paralleling the topics in Leviticus 24:10-24. Perhaps both Moses and our Lord are saying, "If you have the fear of God in your heart, you won't try to retaliate when people mistreat you." Romans 13:1-7 is God's statement on the

place of human government in society, and 12:14-21 is God's admonition to His people concerning personal insults and attacks.

4. Opponents of capital punishment like to quote statistics to prove that executions are not a deterrent to crime. But using statistics either to defend or oppose capital punishment is a lost cause because there's no possible way to set up a "control" situation to test the statistics. The size and composition of the population of a state or city, plus the local laws and how they are enforced, have considerable bearing on the matter. Even the American humanist lawyer Clarence Darrow, an enemy of capital punishment, had to admit, "It is a question that cannot be proven one way or the other by statistics." During his career, Darrow defended one hundred accused murderers, and not one was executed. See *Lend Me Your Ears: Great Speeches in History,* selected by William Safire (New York: W.W. Norton, 1992), 327–35.

Chapter 11
1. Keep in mind that the Jewish religious year began in April with Passover (Ex. 12:2); their civil year began with the Feast of Trumpets seven months later.

2. The NIV margin reads "take excessive interest," which is what happened in the time of Nehemiah (Neh. 5). However, the rabbis interpreted this law to mean interest-free loans.

3. Alexander Maclaren, *The Expositor's Bible,* vol. VI (Grand Rapids: Eerdmans, 1940), 301.

Chapter 12
1. Harris, Archer, and Waltke, eds. *Theological Wordbook of the Old Testament,* vol. 2 (Chicago: Moody Press, 1980), 814.

Chapter 13
1. Carl F.H. Henry, *Notes on the Doctrine of God* (Boston: W.A. Wilde, 1948), 110.